1001
DUMBEST
THINGS
EVER SAID

ALSO BY THE AUTHOR

Teaching Riding at Summer Camp
Panorama of American Horses
Civil Rights (Vols. 1 & 2)
Get a Horse!
Take Me Home
The Second-Time Single Man's Survival Handbook
Old as the Hills
Horseback Vacation Guide
Schooling to Show
The Whole Horse Catalog
Riding's a Joy
All the King's Horses
The Beautiful Baby Naming Book
Riding for a Fall
The Polo Primer
The Ultimate Fishing Guide
Caught Me a Big 'Un
The Complete Book of the American Quarter Horse
Two Bits' Book of the American Quarter Horse
Essential Riding
The Illustrated Horseman's Dictionary
The Greatest Horse Stories Ever Told
Classic Horse Stories

1001
DUMBEST
THINGS
EVER SAID

Edited and with an Introduction by

Steven D. Price

THE LYONS PRESS
Guilford, Connecticut
An imprint of The Globe Pequot Press

The Lyons Press is an imprint of The Globe Pequot Press

10 9 8 7 6 5 4 3 2 1

Printed in the United States of America

Designed by Carol Sawyer/Rose Design

ISBN 1-59228-787-5

The Library of Congress has previously published an earlier (hardcover) edition as follows:

1001 dumbest things ever said / edited and with an introduction by Steven D. Price.
   p. cm.
   ISBN 1-59228-267-9 (trade cloth)
   1. Quotations, English. I. Title: One thousand one dumbest things ever said. II. Title: One thousand and one dumbest things ever said. III. Price, Steven D.

PN6081.A1258 2004
082—dc22

2004048958

CONTENTS

When more and more people are thrown out of work, unemployment results.

—Calvin Coolidge

INTRODUCTION

*H*istory does not reveal the identity of the first person to say something dumb. It might have been a caveman who approached a saber-toothed tiger with "nice kitty." Or who confidently confided to a neighbor that the newfangled "wheel" gizmo would never replace good old-fashioned walking.

We'll never know, but we can say with some assurance that based on recorded history, dumb remarks have been with us since the invention of writing. Young or old, rich or poor, famous or unknown, people of all generations and cultures have seized the opportunity to say something dumb—stupidity has always been an equal opportunity employer.

What makes something dumb? An essential element, and perhaps *the* essential element, is—paradoxically—superior knowledge. In the above example, the caveman might not have known that saber-toothed tigers aren't harmless felines, but we do: the gap between what the caveman knew (or thought he knew) and what we in fact know provides the entertainment factor.

Speaking of knowledge, the greater the expectation that the speaker knows or should know something, the greater the "dumbness" value. There's nothing inherently foolish about laymen doubting the effectiveness or utility of an item, as in the "it'll never get off the ground" or "get a horse" response to the first airplane or automobile.

However, it's quite another thing for a rear admiral to say, as one did in 1939, that "As far as sinking a ship with a bomb is concerned, you just can't do it." Or, similarly, IBM's chairman of the board predicting in 1943: "I think there is a world market for maybe five computers." Scattered throughout this book, you will encounter various members of our very own Hall of Shame: people whose moments of verbal neglect, logical inconsistency, or plain-and-simple stupidity have been so frequent that they deserve special recognition. Ranging from presidents of countries and corporations to experienced sports commentators, these are folks who really ought to have known better.

Politics has always been a fertile field for misstatements and outright foolishness, primarily because elected and appointed officials spend far too much time talking, and the more one talks, the greater the opportunity is to say the wrong thing. Then too, trying to be all things to all people—or constituents—leaves political figures open to statements that can come back to haunt them. And it's not just the George W. Bushes, Dan Quayles, and Al Gores of the world: even Abraham Lincoln ("People who like this sort of thing will find this the sort of thing they like"), Dwight Eisenhower ("Things are more like they are now than they ever were before"), and Charles de Gaulle ("China is a big country, inhabited by many Chinese") had their lapses.

Radio, television, magazines, newspapers, and Web commentators point with great glee to the misstatements of public figures, but members of the media are equally likely to say or print something dumb. For example, veteran radio announcer Lowell Thomas presenting the British politician, Sir Stafford Cripps, as "Sir Stifford Craps." Ambiguous newspaper headlines (PLANE TOO CLOSE TO GROUND, CRASH PROBE TOLD and MINERS REFUSE TO WORK AFTER DEATH) make us laugh. So do supermodels ("I don't diet. I just don't eat as much as I'd like to"— Linda Evangelista) and super-producers ("Television has raised writing to a new low"—Samuel Goldwyn).

There must be something about sports that causes as many errors to be made in the broadcast booth or locker room as on the playing field. Leading the baseball all-star lineup are the incomparable Yogi Berra ("You give 100 percent in the first half of the game, and if that isn't enough, in the second half you give what's left") and Casey Stengel ("Good pitching will always stop good hitting and vice versa"), but hard on their heels are Jerry Coleman ("There is someone warming up in the Giants' bullpen, but he's obscured by his number") and Ralph Kiner ("The Mets have gotten their leadoff batter on only once this inning"). Other sports are part of the blooper hit parade, from basketball ("We're going to turn this team around 360 degrees"—the New Jersey Nets's Jason Kidd) to golf ("And now to hole eight, which is in fact the eighth hole"—commentator Peter Alliss) to boxing ("I was in a no-win situation, so I'm glad that I won rather than lost."—Frank Bruno).

Literature has abounded in goofs, from spoonerism linguistic leapfrogs ("a blushing crow" instead of "a crushing blow") to malapropisms ("She's as headstrong as an allegory on the banks of the Nile"). And on a less literary and far less literate level, students of all ages and any and all disciplines have come up with jaw-droppers of their own: "Moses went up on Mount Cyanide to get the Ten Commandments" or "Never look a gift horse in the mouse."

The 1001 nuggets found between these covers have been collected and culled from radio, television, books, newspapers, magazines, and Web sites. Many are well known, as are the people who uttered or wrote them. Others are far less so—to the point, some might say, of being apocryphal, especially the more outrageously idiotic entries. That raises the question of authenticity, which can be best answered by saying that to the best of someone's knowledge, everything herein was actually said.

How can that be? the curious reader might wonder—could anyone have been that dumb?

Let me respectfully answer with another question: Is there anyone among us who has never said anything that, whether intentional or inadvertent, could be classified as dumb? We all have, so while you snicker, chuckle, or belly-laugh through this book, remember that those who are without sin, stone the first cast . . . er, cast the first stone.

STEVEN D. PRICE
NEW YORK, NEW YORK
MAY 2004

POLITICS

I've read about foreign policy and studied; I now know the number of continents.

—*George Wallace, in his 1968 presidential campaign*

Thanks for the poncho.

—*Bill Clinton, when presented with the Romanian tricolor flag during a visit to that country*

It has not worked. No one can say it has worked, so I decided we're either going to do what we said we're going to do with the UN, or we're going to do something else.

—*Bill Clinton, on the UN operation in Bosnia*

You know, if I were a single man, I might ask that mummy out.
That's a good-looking mummy!
>   —*Bill Clinton, referring to an excavated Inca mummy*

As I was telling my husb— . . . As I was telling President Bush . . .
>   —*Condoleezza Rice, unmarried national security advisor*

It's not true the Congressman was sleeping during the debate. He
was just taking a few moments for deep reflection.
>   —*aide to Rep. Martin Hoke, who was spotted on the House of
>   Representatives floor with eyes closed during a debate*

I think we're on the road to coming up with answers that I don't think any of us in total feel we have the answers to.

—Kim Anderson, mayor of Naples, Florida

You reporters should have printed what he meant, not what he said.

—Earl Bush, aide to Chicago mayor Richard Daley

A proof is a proof. What kind of a proof? It's a proof. A proof is a proof. And when you have a good proof, it's because it's proven.

—Jean Chrétien

Give Bill a second term, and Al Gore and I will be turned loose to do what we really want to do.
   —*Hillary Clinton, speaking at a 1996 Democratic fund-raiser*

We've got a strong candidate. I'm trying to think of his name.
                                    —*Senator Christopher Dodd*

H
A
L
L

O
F

S
H
A
M
E

HALL OF SHAME MEMBER #1

George W. Bush, the forty-third president of the United States, has become infamous for his ability to spend a lot of time saying very little. The following are a very select few of his hundreds of brilliantly dumb statements:

I think we can agree. The past is over.

[Senator John McCain] . . . can't have it both ways. He can't take the high horse and then claim the low road.

If you're sick and tired of the politics of cynicism and polls and principles, come and join this campaign.

It's no exaggeration to say that the undecided could go one way or another.

Oftentimes, we live in a processed world; you know, people focus on the process and not results.

The law I sign today directs new funds . . . to the task of collecting vital intelligence . . . on weapons of mass production.

It will take time to restore chaos and order.

They have miscalculated me as a leader.

Natural gas is hemispheric . . . because it is a product that we can find in our neighborhoods.

I am mindful not only of preserving executive powers for myself, but for predecessors as well.

We need an energy bill that encourages consumption.

We cannot let terrorists and rogue nations hold this nation hostile or hold our allies hostile.

We are making steadfast progress.

H
A
L
L

O
F

S
H
A
M
E

The Internet is a gateway to get on the Net.

—*Bob Dole, former senator*

Things are more like they are now than they ever were before.

—*Dwight D. Eisenhower*

If the King's English was good enough for Jesus, it's good enough for me!

—*Ma Ferguson, former governor of Texas*

Beginning in February 1976, your assistance benefits will be discontinued. Reason: It has been reported to our office that you expired on January 1, 1976.

> —*from a letter by Illinois Department of Public Aid*

China is a big country, inhabited by many Chinese.

> —*Charles de Gaulle, former president of France*

Poultry waste . . . is something that continues to threaten our country.

> —*Tom Daschle, senator from South Dakota*

You always write it's bombing, bombing, bombing. It's not bombing, it's air support.

> —*David Opfer, U.S. Air Force colonel, criticizing reporters'*
> *coverage of the Vietnam War*

A zebra cannot change its spots.

> —*Al Gore*

I tell you, that Michael Jackson is unbelievable, isn't he? Three plays in twenty seconds!

> —*Al Gore, commenting on basketball star Michael Jordan*

People who like this sort of thing will find this the sort of thing they like.

—*Abraham Lincoln*

We do not have censorship. What we have is a limitation on what newspapers can report.

—*Louis Nel, deputy foreign minister from South Africa*

I'm not indecisive. Am I indecisive?

—*Jim Scheibel, mayor of St. Paul, Minnesota*

It's not easy getting up here and saying nothing. It takes a lot of preparation.

—Barry Toiv, White House spokesman

I'm not going to have some reporters pawing through our papers. We are the president.

—Hillary Clinton

That low-down scoundrel deserves to be kicked to death by a jackass, and I'm just the one to do it.

—unidentified Texas congressional candidate

HALL OF SHAME MEMBER #2

Marion Barry, former mayor of Washington, D.C., is famous for his ability to mix up his words. Talk about mangling the language!

I am providing you with a copulation of answers to several questions raised . . .

What we have here is an egregemous miscarriagement of taxitude.

The contagious people of Washington have stood firm against diversity during this long period of increment weather.

I promise you a police car on every sidewalk.

I am making this trip to Africa because Washington is an international city, just like Tokyo, Nigeria, or Israel. As mayor, I am an international symbol. Can you deny that to Africa?

What right does Congress have to go around making laws just because they deem it necessary?

Outside of the killings, Washington has one of the lowest crime rates in the country.

People blame me because these water mains break, but I ask you, if the water mains didn't break, would it be my responsibility to fix them then? Would it?

I read a funny story about how the Republicans freed the slaves. The Republicans are the ones who created slavery by law in the 1600s. Abraham Lincoln freed the slaves and he was not a Republican.

There are two kinds of truth. There are real truths, and there are made-up truths.

I am a great mayor; I am an upstanding Christian man; I am an intelligent man; I am a deeply educated man; I am a humble man.

It isn't pollution that's harming the environment. It's the impurities in our air and water that are doing it.

—Dan Quayle

I was provided with additional input that was radically different from the truth. I assisted in furthering that version.

—Colonel Oliver North, from his Iran-Contra testimony

During my service in the United States Congress, I took the initiative in creating the Internet.

—Al Gore

We don't necessarily discriminate. We simply exclude certain types
of people.

—Colonel Gerald Wellman, ROTC instructor

If we don't succeed, we run the risk of failure.

—Bill Clinton

We are ready for an unforeseen event that may or may not occur.

—Al Gore

In every country the Communists have taken over, the first thing they do is outlaw cockfighting.

> *—John Monks, state representative from Oklahoma, arguing against a bill to outlaw cockfighting in his state*

Attaboy, Senator! Atta—uh, girl . . . person . . . what are you anyway?

> *—Senator Jesse Helms addressing a female colleague*

Traditionally, most of Australia's imports come from overseas.

> *—Keppel Enderbery, former Australian cabinet minister*

Facts are stupid things.

—Ronald Reagan

My fellow Americans, I've signed legislation that will outlaw Russia forever. We begin bombing in five minutes.

—Ronald Reagan, unaware a radio microphone was on

I favor the Civil Rights Act of 1964 and it must be enforced at gunpoint if necessary.

—Ronald Reagan

I would have voted against the Civil Rights Act of 1964.

—Ronald Reagan

There is a mandate to impose a voluntary return to traditional values.
                                                    —*Ronald Reagan*

I don't intend for this to take on a political tone. I'm just here for
the drugs.
                        —*Nancy Reagan, speaking at an anti-drug rally*

Your food stamps will be stopped effective March 1992 because we
received notice that you passed away. May God bless you. You may
reapply if there is a change in your circumstances.
        —*Department of Social Services, Greenville, South Carolina*

If somebody has a bad heart, they can plug this jack in at night as they go to bed and it will monitor their heart throughout the night. And the next morning, when they wake up dead, there'll be a record.
> —*Mark S. Fowler, FCC chairman*

Marriage is something that should be between a man and a woman.
> —*Arnold Schwarzenegger, California governor*

Having committed political suicide, the Conservative Party is now living to regret it.
> —*Chris Patten, British politician*

Sure, [pesticides] are going to kill a lot of people, but they may be dying of something else anyway.

   —*Othal Brand, member of Texas pesticide review board*

We have every mixture you can think of. I have a black, I have a woman, two Jews, and a cripple.

   —*James Watt, Secretary of the Interior,*
       on the diversity of his staff

Honest businessmen should be protected from the unscrupulous consumer.

   —*Lester Maddox, governor of Georgia, arguing against the*
     creation of a state consumer protection agency

He's trying to take the decision out of the hands of twelve honest men and give it to congressmen!
> —*Charles Vanik, Ohio congressman, reacting to former Vice President Agnew's request to have his corruption case tried by the House of Representatives*

In the early sixties, we were strong, we were virulent . . .
> —*John Connally, Secretary of the Treasury under Richard Nixon*

The streets are safe in Philadelphia; it's only the people who make them unsafe.
> —*Frank Rizzo, mayor of Philadelphia*

I've always thought that underpopulated countries in Africa are
vastly underpolluted.

> —*Lawrence Summers, chief economist of the*
> *World Bank, explaining why we should export*
> *toxic wastes to Third World countries*

These people were highly susceptible to homicide. We know that
because they were killed.

> —*Paul Blackman, research coordinator at the National*
> *Rifle Association, criticizing a study showing that*
> *guns in the home are found to increase risk of death*

I can't believe that we are going to let a majority of the people
decide what is best for this state.

> —*John Travis, representative from Louisiana*

The Knights of Peter Claver is a large Catholic organization.
                    —*Wilfred Pierre, representative from Louisiana*

I'm a large Catholic, and I don't belong to it.
                    —*Juba Diez, representative from Louisiana*

I don't know anyone here that's been killed with a handgun.
                    —*Rep. Avery Alexander, D-New Orleans,*
                              to the House of Representatives

This amendment does more damage than it does harm.
                    —*Cynthia Willard-Lewis, representative from Louisiana*

I think we have passed something that we didn't want to do.

>   —*Chuck McMains, representative from Louisiana*

Y'all are hurting my tender ears. I would appreciate it if y'all would scream one at a time.

>   —*John Alario, House Speaker from Louisiana*

I am honored today to begin my first term as the governor of Baltimore—that is, Maryland.

>   —*William Schaefer*

I now have absolute proof that smoking even one marijuana cigarette is equal in brain damage to being on Bikini Island during an H-bomb blast.

—Ronald Reagan

Now we are trying to get unemployment to go up, and I think we're going to succeed.

—Ronald Reagan

The President has kept all of the promises he intended to keep.

—Clinton White House aide George Stephanopoulos

When more and more people are thrown out of work, unemployment results.

—Calvin Coolidge

If you let that sort of thing go on, your bread and butter will be cut right out from under your feet.

—Ernest Bevin, British foreign minister

I'm not against the blacks, and a lot of the good blacks will attest to that.

—Evan Mecham, governor of Arizona

Nixon has been sitting in the White House while George McGovern has been exposing himself to the people of the United States.
                    —*Frank Licht, governor of Rhode Island*

I haven't committed a crime. What I did was fail to comply with the law.
                    —*David Dinkins, mayor of New York City*

They gave me a book of checks. They didn't ask for any deposits.
                    —*Joe Early, Massachusetts congressman,*
                                on the House bank scandal

He [President Bush] didn't say that. He was reading what was given to him in a speech.
—*Richard Darman, Office of Management and Budget director*

$\sim$

I didn't accept it. I received it.
—*Richard Allen, Reagan White House national security advisor, explaining gifts given by two Japanese journalists after he helped arrange a private interview with Nancy Reagan*

$\sim$

I was a pilot flying an airplane and it just so happened that where I was flying made what I was doing spying.
—*Francis Gary Power, reconnaissance pilot captured by the Soviets*

$\sim$

I regret to say that we of the FBI are powerless to act in cases of oral-genital intimacy, unless it has in some way obstructed interstate commerce.

—J. Edgar Hoover, FBI director

The Maastricht Treaty . . . has been dealt, at least temporarily, a fatal blow.

—Des O'Malley, Irish government minister

In the words of George Bernard Shaw, "Two roads diverged in a wood, and I—I took the one less traveled by."

—Indiana governor Evan Bayh, misquoting and misidentifying Robert Frost, in a speech calling for educational excellence given at a meeting of the Indiana Educational Committee

I'm running for president of the United States because I believe that—with strong leadership—America's days will always lie ahead of us. Just as they lie ahead of us now.

—*Bob Dole*

Those who survived the San Francisco earthquake said, "Thank God, I'm still alive." But of course, those who died—their lives will never be the same again.

—*Barbara Boxer, representative from California*

Capital punishment is our society's recognition of the sanctity of human life.

—*Orrin G. Hatch, senator from Utah*

Democracy used to be a good thing, but now it has gotten into the wrong hands.

—*Jesse Helms, senator from North Carolina*

But we are not about to send American boys nine or ten thousand miles away from home to do what Asian boys ought to be doing for themselves.

—*Lyndon B. Johnson*

The United States has much to offer the third world war.

—*Ronald Reagan, repeating this mistake nine times in the same address*

We are not without accomplishment. We have managed to distribute poverty equally.

—Nguyen Co Thach, Vietnamese foreign minister

Sure, I look like a white man. But my heart is as black as anyone's here.

—George Wallace, governor of Alabama, to a predominantly African-American audience

Bill Weld will not tiptoe around Washington, D.C. on bended knee.

—William Weld, Massachusetts governor

HALL OF SHAME MEMBER #3

Dan Quayle, vice president under President George H. W. Bush, is perhaps better known for his verbal blunders than for his politics. Let us pause and remember the good ol' days of the first Bush administration, when men were men and a potato was a potatoe.

A low voter turnout is an indication of fewer people going to the polls.

Mars is essentially in the same orbit. Mars is somewhat the same distance from the sun, which is very important. We have seen pictures where there are canals, we believe, and water. If there is water, that means there is oxygen. If oxygen, that means we can breathe.

Republicans understand the importance of bondage between a mother and child.

I stand by all my misstatements.

Rural Americans are real Americans. There's no doubt about that. You can't always be sure with other Americans. Not all of them are real.

One word sums up probably the responsibility of any vice president. And that one word is "to be prepared."

What a waste it is to lose one's mind. Or not to have a mind is being very wasteful. How true that is.

Hawaii has always been a very pivotal role in the Pacific. It is in the Pacific. It is a part of the United States that is an island that is right here.

I have made good judgments in the past. I have made good judgments in the future.

My friends, no matter how rough the road may be, we can and we will never, never surrender to what is right.

I believe we are on an irreversible trend toward more freedom and democracy. But that could change.

H
A
L
L

O
F

S
H
A
M
E

The Holocaust was an obscene period in our nation's history . . . this century's history. . . . We all lived in this century. I didn't live in this century.

We have a firm commitment to NATO, we are a part of NATO. We have a firm commitment to Europe. We are a part of Europe.

The United States will work toward the elimination of human rights.
                                        —in a pledge to El Salvador

I love California. I practically grew up in Phoenix.

I would not have married Dan Quayle had I not thought he was an equal to me.

—*Marilyn Quayle*

The Jews and Arabs should settle their dispute in the true spirit of Christian charity.

—*Alexander Wiley, senator from Wisconsin*

This is unparalyzed in the state's history.

—*Gib Lewis, Texas Speaker of the House*

The best cure for insomnia is to get a lot of sleep.

—Senator S. I. Hayakawa

The police are not here to create disorder, they're here to preserve disorder.

—Richard Daley, former mayor of Chicago

He was a man of great statue.

—Thomas Menino, former mayor of Boston

We are getting into semantics again. If we use words, there is a very grave danger they will be misinterpreted.

—H. R. Haldemn

Justice is incidental to law and order.

—J. EdgarHoover

We were at war. They were an endangered species.

*—Howard Coble, representative from North Carolina,
insisting that the internment of Japanese-Americans
during World War II was for their own protection*

[Osama bin Laden] is either alive and well, or alive and not well, or not alive.

—*Donald Rumsfeld, secretary of defense*

I understand it's a nice lifestyle. I love golf, and I understand they have a lot of nice golf courses.

—*Chic Hecht, senator from Nevada, on why he should be appointed ambassador to the Bahamas*

HALL OF SHAME MEMBER #4

Following the Watergate scandal, the name Richard Nixon became almost synonymous with government corruption. We discovered that not only was Nixon corrupt, but he also had a flair for saying the wrong thing at the wrong time—with a tape recorder running.

This is a great day for France!
>   *—while attending the funeral of Charles de Gaulle*

I was not lying. I said things that later on seemed to be untrue.
>   *—discussing Watergate in 1978*

It is necessary for me to establish a winner image. Therefore, I have to beat somebody.

If you think the United States has stood still, who built the largest shopping center in the world?

When I grow up, I want to be an honest lawyer so things like that [the Teapot Dome scandal] can't happen.

Sure, there are dishonest men in local government. But there are dishonest men in national government too.

When the president does it, that means it is not illegal.

I would have made a good pope.

Nothing would please the Kremlin more than to have the people of this country choose a second-rate president.

Voters quickly forget what a man says.

If a cricketer suddenly decided to go into a school and batter a lot of people to death with a cricket bat—which he could do very easily—I mean, are you going to ban cricket bats?

> —*Prince Philip, reacting to proposals to ban firearms*

If it has got four legs and isn't a chair, if it has got two wings and isn't a plane, and if it swims and isn't a submarine, the Cantonese will eat it.

> —*Prince Philip*

Everybody was saying we must have more leisure. Now they are complaining they are unemployed.

> —*Prince Philip, during the 1981 recession*

You are a woman, aren't you?

—Prince Philip, in Kenya, 1984,
after accepting a gift from a native woman

Deaf? If you were near there, no wonder you are deaf.

—Prince Philip, to deaf people near a steel band

If you stay here much longer you'll be slitty-eyed.

—Prince Philip, to British students in China

One of our nation's greatest leaders was Hubert Horatio
Hornblower . . .

> —*Jimmy Carter, referring to Vice President*
> *Hubert Horatio Humphrey in Carter's 1978*
> *presidential nomination acceptance speech*

George Bush doesn't have the manhood to apologize.

> —*Walter Mondale*

Well, on the manhood thing, I'll put mine up against his any time.

> —*George H. W. Bush*

The exports include thumbscrews and cattle prods, just routine
items for the police.

> —*a Commerce Department spokesman on*
> *allowing the export of various products*

After finding no qualified candidates for the position of principal, the school department is extremely pleased to announce the appointment of David Steele to the post.

—*Philip Streifer, superintendent of schools,*
Barrington, Rhode Island

President Carter speaks loudly and carries a fly spotter, a fly swasher—it's been a long day.

—*Gerald Ford*

Wait a minute! I'm not interested in agriculture. I want the military stuff.

—*William Scott, senator from Virginia,*
when he was told about missile silos

I am a jelly doughnut.

> —*English translation of John F. Kennedy's "Ich bin ein berliner" line at the Berlin Wall ["I am a Berliner" is, in correct German, "Ich bin berliner"—the ein makes the sentence refer to a berliner, a type of pastry]*

Without censorship, things can get terribly confused in the public mind.

> —*General William Westmoreland*

It depends on your definition of "asleep." They were not stretched out. They had their eyes closed. They were seated at their desks with their heads in a nodding position.

> —*John Hogan, plant official, responding to a charge that two nuclear plant operators were sleeping on the job*

The chances of Amsterdam becoming a car-free city are as big as the chances of me getting involved in a relationship. If it might ever come to that, I'll calculate what it is going to cost me and I will not go through with it after all.

> —*a Dutch politician reacting to a question about whether autos should be banned from the center of the city*

We must rise to higher and higher platitudes together.

> —*Richard J. Daley, mayor of Chicago*

If I seem unduly clear to you, you must have misunderstood what I said.

> —*Alan Greenspan, Federal Reserve chairman*

Now, like, I'm President. It would be pretty hard for some drug guy to come into the White House and start offering it up, you know? . . . I bet if they did, I hope I would say, "Hey, get lost. We don't want any of that."

—*George H.W. Bush*

For seven and a half years I've worked alongside President Reagan. We've had triumphs. Made some mistakes. We've had some sex . . . uh . . . setbacks.

—*George H.W. Bush*

The caribou love it [the Alaska pipeline]. They rub against it and they have babies. There are more caribou in Alaska than you can shake a stick at.

—*George H.W. Bush*

HALL OF SHAME MEMBER #5

Sir Boyle Roche was an eighteenth–century Irish member of Parliament noted for malapropisms and other gaffes:

Mr. Speaker, I smell a rat; I see him forming in the air and darkening the sky; but I'll nip him in the bud.

A man could not be in two places at the same time unless he were a bird.

Half the lies our opponents tell about us are untrue.

I concluded from the beginning that this would be the end; and I am right, for it is not half over.

The cup of Ireland's misery has been overflowing for centuries, and is not yet half full.

Ireland and England are like two sisters; I would have them embrace like one brother.

Every pint bottle should contain a quart.

It would surely be better to give up, not only a part but, if necessary, the whole of our constitution, to preserve the remainder.

I answer in the affirmative with an emphatic "No."

We should silence anyone who opposes the right to freedom of speech.

Many of them were destitute of even the goods they possessed.

While I write this letter, I have a pistol in one hand and a sword in the other.

All along the untrodden paths of the future I can see the footprints of an unseen hand.

He is the kind of opponent who would stab you in front of your face and then stab you in the chest when your back is turned.

HALL OF SHAME

P.S. If you do not receive this, of course it must have been miscarried; therefore, I beg you to write and let me know.

Sir, I would anchor a frigate off each bank of the river, with strict orders not to stir; and so, by cruising up and down, put a stop to smuggling.

I told you to make one longer than the other, and instead you have made one shorter than the other.

The progress of the times . . . [is] . . . such that little children, who can neither walk nor talk, may be seen cursing their Maker!

II.

SPORTS

HALL OF SHAME MEMBER #6

*Few sports figures—and indeed, few figures in any endeavor—have
achieved the verbal notoriety of Lawrence "Yogi" Berra, former catcher
of the New York Yankees. Herewith, a smattering of his indescribable
utterances:*

This is like déjà vu all over again.

You can observe a lot just by watching.

He must have made that [movie] before he died.
                    —*a reference to movie star Steve McQueen*

I'd find the fellow who lost it, and, if he was poor, I'd return it.
    —*when asked what he would do if he found a million dollars.*

Think! How the hell are you gonna think and hit at the same
time?

You've got to be very careful if you don't know where you're going,
because you might not get there.

I knew I was going to take the wrong train, so I left early.

If you can't imitate him, don't copy him.

You better cut the pizza in four pieces because I'm not hungry enough to eat six.

Baseball is 90 percent mental—the other half is physical.

It was impossible to get a conversation going—everybody was talking too much.

Slump? I ain't in no slump. I just ain't hitting.

A nickel isn't worth a dime today.

Nobody goes there anymore—it's too crowded.

It gets late early out there.
> *—a reference to the visual conditions in Yankee Stadium's left field when the setting sun affects playing fly balls*

Surprise me.

*—when his wife asked, "Yogi, you are from St. Louis, we live in
New Jersey, and you played ball in New York. If you go before
I do, where would you like me to have you buried?"*

Do you mean now?

—when asked for the time

I take a two-hour nap, from one o'clock to four.

If you come to a fork in the road, take it.

You give 100 percent in the first half of the game, and if that isn't
enough, in the second half you give what's left.

Ninety percent of the putts that are short don't go in.

I made a wrong mistake.

I always thought that record would stand until it was broken.

Yeah, but we're making great time!

> —*replying to the suggestion that he*
> *and another person were lost*

Why buy good luggage? You only use it when you travel.

It's never happened in the World Series competition, and it still hasn't.

How long have you known me, Jack? And you still don't know how to spell my name.

> —*after receiving a check from*
> *Jack Buck made out to* BEARER

I'd say he's done more than that.

> —*when asked whether infielder Don*
> *Mattingly exceeded expectations*

The other teams could make trouble for us if they win.

He can run anytime he wants. I'm giving him the red light.

I never blame myself when I'm not hitting. I just blame the bat, and if it keeps up, I change bats. After all, if I know it isn't my fault that I'm not hitting, how can I get mad at myself?

It ain't the heat; it's the humility.

You should always go to other people's funerals; otherwise, they won't come to yours.

I don't know. I'm not in shape yet.

—when asked his cap size

I didn't really say everything I said.

HALL OF SHAME MEMBER #7

Charles "Casey" Stengel, Yankees Hall of Fame manager, was another master of obfuscation:

A lot of people my age are dead at the present time.

I was not very good at pulling teeth, but my mother loved my work.
                    —on his early career as a dentist

All right, everybody line up alphabetically according to your height.

I would not admire hitting against Ryne Duren, because if he ever hit you in the head, you might be in the past tense.

Left-handers have more enthusiasm for life. They sleep on the wrong side of the bed and their head gets more stagnant on that side.

As great as the other men were on the ball club, there comes a time when you get a weakness and it might be physical.

H
A
L
L

O
F

S
H
A
M
E

Good pitching will always stop good hitting and vice versa.

I couldn't have done it without my players.

I don't know if he throws a spitball, but he sure spits on the ball.

My health is good enough about the shoulders.

The team has come along slow but fast.

If anyone wants me, tell them I'm being embalmed.

If we're going to win the pennant, we've got to start thinking we're not as good as we think we are.

I got players with bad watches—they can't tell midnight from noon.

It's wonderful to meet so many friends that I didn't used to like.

There comes a time in every man's life, and I've had plenty of them.

They got a lot of kids now whose uniforms are so tight, especially the pants, that they cannot bend over to pick up ground balls. And they don't want to bend over in television games because in that way, there is no way their face can get on the camera.

You have to have a catcher, or you'll have all passed balls.

They say he's [Yogi Berra] funny. Well, he has a lovely wife and family, a beautiful home, money in the bank, and he plays golf with millionaires. What's funny about that?

HALL OF SHAME MEMBER #8

Jerry Coleman was an infielder for the Yankees (what is it about the Bronx Bombers that turned out such a raft of funny speakers?), and manager of the San Diego Padres. After playing, he made his mark as a radio and TV broadcaster, where his malapropisms, non sequiturs, and other goofs became legendary.

Mike Caldwell, the Padres's right-handed southpaw, will pitch tonight.

Rich Folkers is throwing up in the bull pen.

Billy Almon has all of his in-law and outlaws here this afternoon.

Sometimes big trees grow out of acorns—I think I heard that from a squirrel.

That's the fourth extra base hit for the Padres—two doubles and a triple.

And Kansas City is at Chicago tonight, or is that Chicago at Kansas City? Well, no matter; Kansas City leads in the eighth, 4 to 4.

[Manny] Sanguillen is totally unpredictable to pitch to because he's so unpredictable.

At the end, excitement maintained its hysteria.

The new Haitian baseball can't weigh more than four ounces, or less than five.

The way he's swinging the bat, he won't get a hit until the twentieth century.

That noise in my earphones knocked my nose off, and I had to pick it up and find it.

I've made a couple of mistakes I'd like to do over.

A day without newspapers is like walking around without your pants on.

Thomas is racing for it, but McCovey is there and can't get his glove to it. That play shows the inexperience, not on Thomas's part, but on the part of Willie McC . . . well, not on McCovey's part, either.

Jesus Alou is in the on-deck circus.

There is someone warming up in the Giants's bullpen, but he's obscured by his number.

HALL OF SHAME

If Pete Rose brings the Reds in first, they ought to bronze him and put him in cement.

They throw Winfield out at second, but he's safe.

Ozzie makes a leaping, diving stop, shovels to Fernando, and everybody drops everything.

Johnny Grubb slides into second with a stand-up double.

All the Padres need is a fly ball in the air.

Davis fouls out to third in fair territory.

Houston has its largest crowd of the night here this evening.

Montreal leads Atlanta by three, 5–1.

How can you communicate with Enzo Hernandez when he speaks Spanish and you speak Mexican?

—asked of Hector Torrez

Hi folks, I'm Jerry Gross . . . Coleman!

HALL OF SHAME MEMBER #9

Ralph Kiner, Pittsburgh Pirates Hall of Fame slugger, has been a radio and television broadcast voice of the New York Mets since 1962. With lines like these, may he continue for another four decades:

Kevin McReynolds stops at third and he scores.

The Mets have gotten their leadoff batter on only once this inning.

There is a lot of heredity in that family.

The reason the Mets have played so well at Shea this year is they have the best home record in baseball.

The Hall of Fame ceremonies are on the 31st and 32nd of July.

After eight innings, it's the New York Giants—who have moved to San Francisco—4, and the Mets, 3.

H
A
L
L

O
F

S
H
A
M
E

[Don] Sutton lost 13 games in a row without winning a ball game.

We'll be back after this word from Manufacturer's Hangover.
—the bank's correct name is Manufacturer's Hanover

You have really solidified the Mets's center-field problems.

The Mets just had their first .500-or-better April since July of 1992.

Today is Father's Day, so to all you fathers out there, we'd just like to say, Happy Birthday!

Solo homers usually come with no one on base.

If Casey Stengel were alive today, he'd be spinning in his grave.

Darryl Strawberry has been voted to the Hall of Fame five years in a row.

Tony Gwynn was named player of the year for April.

George Shinn. He's the owner of the Charlotte Harlots basketball team.

> —*Kiner meant to say* Hornets

All of his saves have come in relief appearances.

Ralph Korner.
—*Kiner introducing himself on his postgame show, "Kiner's Korner"*

H
A
L
L

O
F

S
H
A
M
E

BASEBALL

Any pitcher who throws at a batter and deliberately tries to hit him is a Communist.

> —*Alvin Dark, New York Giants infielder*

Well, I see in the game in Minnesota that Terry Felton has relieved himself on the mound in the second inning.

> —*Fred White, Kansas City Royals sportscaster, reading a wire-service summary that erroneously named the same starter and relief pitcher for the Minnesota Twins*

Even Napoleon had his Watergate.

> —*Danny Ozark, Philadelphia Phillies manager*

Folks, this is perfect weather for today's game. Not a breath of air.
                                    —*Curt Gowdy, sports commentator*

If Jesus were on the field, he'd be pitching inside and breaking up double plays. He'd be high-fiving the other guys.
                                    —*Tim Burke, Montreal Expos pitcher*

All I said was that the trades were stupid and dumb, and they took that and blew it all out of proportion.
                                    —*Ron Davis, Minnesota Twins pitcher*

I am throwing twice as hard as I ever did. It's just not getting there as fast.

—Lefty Gomez, New York Yankees pitcher

I was the worst hitter ever. I never even broke a bat until last year when I was backing out of the garage.

—Lefty Gomez

The doctors X-rayed my head and found nothing.

—Dizzy Dean, National League pitcher, after being hit on the head by a ball in the 1934 World Series

I prefer fast food.

—infielder Rocky Bridges, when asked
why he would not eat snails

Her name's Mrs. Coleman. She likes me.
—Choo Choo Coleman, New York Mets catcher, when asked by
Ralph Kiner for his wife's name and what she was like

I dunno. I never smoked any Astroturf.

—Tug McGraw, National League pitcher, when asked
whether he preferred grass or Astroturf

Always root for the winner. That way you won't be disappointed.

—*Tug McGraw*

I told [General Manager] Roland Hemond to go out and get me a big-name pitcher. He said, "Dave Wehrmeister's got eleven letters. Is that a big enough name for you?"

—*Eddie Eichorn, Chicago White Sox owner*

Raise the urinals.

—*Darrel Chaney, Atlanta Braves infielder,
on how to keep the Braves on their toes*

They shouldn't throw at me. I'm the father of five or six kids.

—Tito Fuentes, National League infielder

I'm a four-wheel-drive-pickup type of guy. So is my wife.

—Mike Greenwell, Boston Red Sox outfielder

There is one word in America that says it all, and that word is, "You never know."

—Joaquin Andujar, National League pitcher

That's why I don't talk. Because I talk too much.

—*Joaquin Andujar*

Sometimes they write what I say and not what I mean.

—*Pedro Guerrero, National League infielder/outfielder*

Well, that kind of puts a damper on even a Yankee win.

—*Phil Rizzuto, Yankees broadcaster, upon hearing that Pope Paul had died*

I lost it in the sun!

—*Billy Loes, Brooklyn Dodgers pitcher,*
after fumbling a grounder

I want all the kids to do what I do, to look up to me. I want all the kids to copulate me.

—*Andre Dawson, Chicago Cubs outfielder,*
on being a role model

It would take some of the lust off the All-Star game.

—*Pete Rose, Cincinnati Reds infielder/outfielder,*
asked about inter-league play

It could permanently hurt a batter for a long time.
                    —*Pete Rose, describing a brushback pitch*

Me and George and Billy are two of a kind.
                    —*Mickey Rivers, Texas Rangers outfielder, on*
                    his relationship with Yankees owner George
                    Steinbrenner and manager Billy Martin

His [Dwight Gooden's] reputation preceded him before he got here.
                    —*Don Mattingly, New York Yankees infielder*

FOOTBALL

If you can't make the putts and can't get the man in from second on the bottom of the ninth, you're not going to win enough football games in this league, and that's the problem we had today.

—Sam Rutigliano, Cleveland Browns coach

He fakes a bluff.

—Ron Fairly, New York Giants commentator

Men, I want you just thinking of one word all season. One word and one word only: Super Bowl.

—Bill Peterson, Florida State football coach

He [his coach] treats us like men. He lets us wear earrings.

—Torrin Polk, University of Houston receiver

I don't care what the tape says. I didn't say it.

—Ray Malavasi, St. Louis Rams coach

I may be dumb, but I'm not stupid.

—Terry Bradshaw, player/announcer

I'm not allowed to comment on lousy officiating.
>   —*Jim Finks, New Orleans Saints general manager*

Nobody in football should be called a genius. A genius is a guy like Norman Einstein.
>   —*Joe Theismann, player/commentator*

I want to rush for 1,000 or 1,500 yards, whichever comes first.
>   —*George Rogers, New Orleans Saint running back*

BASKETBALL

. . . and referee Richie Powers called the loose bowel foul on
Johnson.

—Frank Herzog, Washington sports announcer

I've never had major knee surgery on any other part of my body.
—Winston Bennett, University of Kentucky basketball forward

Left hand, right hand, it doesn't matter. I'm amphibious.
—Charles Shackleford, North Carolina State player

I've won at every level, except college and pro.
                    —*Shaquille O'Neal, Los Angeles Lakers player*

We're going to turn this team around 360 degrees.
                    —*Jason Kidd, New Jersey Nets player*

Are you any relation to your brother, Marv?
                    —*Leon Wood, New Jersey Nets player,*
                    to Steve Albert, Nets TV commentator

A lot is said about defense, but at the end of the game, the team with the most points wins—the other team loses.

—*Isaiah Thomas*

It's almost like we have ESPN.

—*Magic Johnson, Los Angeles Lakers player, referring to how well teammate James Worthy and he play together*

I can't really remember the names of the clubs that we went to.

—*Shaquille O'Neal, Los Angeles Lakers player, on whether he had visited the Parthenon during a trip to Greece*

My sister's expecting a baby, and I don't know if I'm going to be
an uncle or an aunt.

> —*Chuck Nevitt, North Carolina State basketball player,*
> *on why he appeared nervous at practice*

Tom.

> —*Tom Nissalke, coach of the Houston Rockets,*
> *when asked how he pronounced his name*

I'll always be Number 1 to myself.

> —*Moses Malone, Philadelphia 76ers player*

I'm going to graduate on time, no matter how long it takes.
                    —*unnamed basketball senior, University of Pittsburgh*

SOCCER

If we played like that every week, we wouldn't be so inconsistent.
                                        —*Bryan Robson*

It's now 1–1, an exact reversal of the score on Saturday.
                                        —*Radio 5 Live*

And Arsenal now have plenty of time to dictate the last few
seconds.

—Peter Jones

. . . and some 500 Italians make the trip, in a crowd of only 400.

—David Smith

Newcastle, of course, unbeaten in their last five wins.

—Brian Moore

Strangely, in slow-motion replay, the ball seemed to hang in the air for even longer.

—*David Acfield*

What I said to them at halftime would be unprintable on the radio.

—*Gerry Francis*

If there weren't such a thing as football, we'd all be frustrated footballers.

—*Mick Lyons*

He's one of those footballers whose brains are in his head.

—Derek Johnstone

The crowd thinks that Todd handled the ball—they must have seen something that nobody else did.

—Barry Davies

Well, either side could win it, or it could be a draw.

—Ron Atkinson, soccer player

Both of the Villa scorers—Withe and Mortimer—were born in Liverpool, as was the Villa manager, Ron Saunders, who was born in Birkenhead.

—David Coleman, commentator

Horse Racing and Other Equestrian Sports

I don't have any immediate thoughts at the moment.

—Walter Swinburn, British jockey, when asked about his immediate thoughts

[Jockey] Steve Cauthen, well on his way to that mythical 200 mark.

—Jimmy Lindley, commentator

A racing horse is not like a machine. It has to be tuned up like a racing car.

—*Chris Pool, commentator*

These two horses have met five times this season, and I think they've beaten each other on each occasion.

—*Jimmy Lindley*

. . . in 1900 the owner of the Grand National winner was the then Prince of Wales, King Edward VII.

—*David Coleman, commentator*

There's Pam watching anxiously. She doesn't look anxious, though.
    —*Stephen Hadley, British show jumper/commentator*

[Jockey] Tony [McCoy] has a quick look between his legs and likes what he sees.
    —*Stewart Machin*

As you travel the world, do you do a lot of traveling ?
    —*Harvey Smith, asked of show jumper*

He's a very competitive competitor, that's the sort of competitor he is.
—*Dorian Williams, horse show commentator*

My horse was in the lead, coming down the homestretch, but the caddie fell off.
—*Samuel Goldwyn, movie producer*

The racecourse is as level as a billiard ball.
—*John Francombe, former jockey*

Golf

There he stands with his legs akimbo.

—*Peter Alliss, commentator*

And now to hole eight, which is in fact the eighth hole.

—*Peter Alliss*

This is the 12th—the green is like a plateau with the top shaved off.

—*Renton Laidlaw, golf writer/commentator*

He used to be fairly indecisive, but now he's not so certain.

—*Peter Alliss*

I owe a lot to my parents, especially my mother and my father.

—*Greg Norman*

I'm a golfer—not an athlete.

—*Lee Westwood*

Arnie [Palmer], usually a great putter, seems to be having trouble with his long putt. However, he has no trouble dropping his shorts.

—*uncredited broadcaster*

TRACK AND FIELD

She hasn't run faster than herself before.

—said of Zola Budd

Born in America, John returned to his native Japan.

—Mike Gratton, commentator

. . . and finally, she tastes the sweet smell of success.

—Ian Edwards, commentator

A very powerful set of lungs, very much hidden by that chest of his.

—Alan Pascoe, commentator

Britain's last gold medal was a bronze in 1952 in Helsinki.

—*Nigel Starmer-Smith, commentator*

The Americans sowed the seed, and now they have reaped the whirlwind.

—*Sebastian Coe, runner*

Well Phil, tell us about your amazing third leg.

—*Ross King, discussing relays with champion runner Phil Redmond*

Mary Decker Slaney, the world's greatest front-runner—I shouldn't be surprised to see her at the front.

—*Ron Pickering, commentator*

Watch the time. It gives you an indication of how fast they are running.

—*Ron Pickering*

And the mile once again becomes the focal point, where it's always been.

—*Ron Pickering*

The Americans' heads are on their chins a little bit at the moment.

—*Ron Pickering*

That's inches away from being millimeter-perfect.

—*Ted Lowe*

HALL OF SHAME MEMBER #10

Great Britain's David Coleman, perhaps a distant relative of American baseball commentator Jerry Coleman, has come up with some prize-winning lines in his track and field commentary:

Don't tell those coming in the final result of that fantastic match, but let's just have another look at Italy's winning goal.

For those of you watching who do not have television sets, live commentary is on Radio 2.

This is a truly international field—no Britons involved.

He won the bronze medal in the 1976 Olympics, so he's used to being out in front.

The late start is due to the time.

He's got his hands on his knees and holds his head in despair.

He's even smaller in real life than he is on the track.

This could be a repeat of what will happen in the European games next week.

It's a battle with himself and with the ticking fingers of the clock.

Here are some names to look forward to—perhaps in the future.

In the Moscow Olympics, Lasse Viren came in fifth and ran a champion's race.

He just can't believe what's not happening to him.

One of the great unknown champions because very little is known about him.

There'll be only one winner now—in every sense.

The Republic of China—back in the Olympic Games for the first time.

That's the fastest time ever run—but it's not as fast as the world record.

He is accelerating all the time. That last lap was run in 64 seconds, and the one before in 62.

It's a great advantage to be able to hurdle with both legs.

And here's Moses Kiptanui, the 19-year-old Kenyan, who turned 20 a few weeks ago.

This evening is a very different evening from the morning that we had this morning.

There's going to be a real ding-dong when the bell goes.

There is Brendan Foster, by himself, with 20,000 people.

We estimate—and this isn't an estimation—that Greta Waitz is 80 seconds behind.

He's 31 this year. Last year he was 30.

There goes Juantorena down the back straight, opening his legs and showing his class.

Morcelli has four fastest 1,500-meter times ever. And all those times are at 1,500 meters.

Her time is about 4.33, which she's capable of.

OTHER SPORTS

And he's got the ice pack on his groin there, so it's possibly not the old shoulder injury.

—*Ray French, rugby sportscaster*

Venezuela! Great, that's the Italian city with the guys in the boats, right?

—*Murad Muhammad, on being told about*
a boxing match in South America

And for those of you watching on black-and-white, the pink ball is the one behind the blue.

—*TV billiards commentator*

I don't want to tell you any half-truths unless they're completely accurate.

—Dennis Rappaport, boxing manager

It's about 90 percent strength and 40 percent technique.
—Johnny Walker, world middleweight wrist-wrestling champion

There isn't a record in existence that hasn't been broken.

—Chay Blyth, yachtsman

It's obvious these Russian swimmers are determined to do well on American soil.

—Anita Lonsborough, commentator

Cycling's a good thing for the youngsters, because it keeps them off the streets.

—David Bean, commentator

In the rear, the small, diminutive figure of Shoaif Mohammed, who can't be much taller or shorter than he is.

—Henry Blofeld, cricket commentator

It's a catch he would have caught 99 times out of 1,000.

—*Henry Blofeld*

His throw went absolutely nowhere near where it was going.

—*Richie Benaud, cricket commentator*

Even Downton couldn't get down high enough for that.

—*Richie Benaud*

That black cloud is coming from the direction the wind is blowing;
now the wind is coming from where the black cloud is.
                    —*Ray Illingworth, former cricket player*

I was in a no-win situation, so I'm glad that I won rather than lost.
                    —*Frank Bruno, boxer*

We now have exactly the same situation as we had at the start of
the race, only exactly the opposite.
                    —*Murray Walker, auto race announcer*

The lead car is absolutely unique, except for the one behind it which is identical.

—*Murray Walker*

There have been injuries and deaths in boxing, but none of them serious.

—*Alan Minter, former prizefighter*

The Queen's Park Oval, exactly as its name suggests, is absolutely round.

—*Tony Crozier, sportscaster*

That's so when I forget how to spell my name, I can still find my
clothes.
>   —*Stu Grimson, Chicago Blackhawks hockey player, on*
>   *why he keeps a color photo of himself above his locker*

We have only one person to blame, and that's each other.
>   —*Barry Beck, New York Ranger, explaining*
>   *a championship game brawl*

If I wasn't talking, I wouldn't know what to say.
>   —*Chico Resch, New York Islanders goalie*

I'm glad you're doing this story on us and not on the WNBA. We're so much prettier than all the other women in sports.

—Martina Hingis, tennis player

It's a nice bonus but, you know, I have to pay taxes too.

—Venus Williams, tennis player,
after winning the Grand Slam Cup

[He] called me a "rapist" and a "recluse." I'm not a recluse.

—Mike Tyson, boxer

He's a guy who gets up at six o'clock in the morning regardless of what time it is.

—Lou Duva, boxing trainer

It's basically the same, just darker.

—Alan Kulwicki, stock car racer, on racing at night instead of during the afternoon

On what?

—boxer Chris Eubank, when asked whether he thought about writing his autobiography

III

SCIENCE, TECHNOLOGY, *AND* BUSINESS

Let's begin with centuries of imperfect views of the future:

ASTRONOMY

Jupiter's moons are invisible to the naked eye, and therefore can have no influence on the earth, and therefore would be useless, and therefore do not exist.

—contemporaries of Galileo Galilei, circa 1610

The proposition, that the sun is the centre and does not revolve about the earth, is foolish, absurd, false in theology and heretical.

—The Inquisition, on Galileo's theories

Comets are not heavenly bodies, but originate in the earth's atmosphere below the moon.

—Father Augustin de Angelis, 1673

MEDICINE

I heard Harvey say that after his book came out, he fell mightily in his practice. 'Twas believed by the vulgar that he was crack-brained, and all the physicians were against him. I knew several doctors in London that would not have given threepence for one of his medicines.

> —*John Aubrey, on the reaction to William Harvey's discovery of blood circulation, circa* 1630

. . . for a man to infect a family in the morning with smallpox and to pray to God in the evening against the disease is blasphemy; that the smallpox is "a judgment of God on the sins of the people," and that "to avert it is but to provoke him more"; that inoculation is "an encroachment on the prerogatives of Jehovah, whose right it is to wound and smite."

> —*contemporary reaction to inoculation experiments by American physician Dr. Zabdiel Boylston, circa* 1720

Smallpox is a visitation from God; but the cowpox is produced by presumptuous man; the former was what Heaven ordained, the latter is, perhaps, a daring violation of our holy religion.
    —*A physician's reaction to Dr. Edward Jenner's experiments in developing a vaccine for smallpox, 1796*

The abolishment of pain in surgery is a chimera. It is absurd to go on seeking it today. "Knife" and "pain" are two words in surgery that must forever be associated in the consciousness of the patient. To this compulsory combination we shall have to adjust ourselves.
    —*Alfred Velpeau, decrying the use of anesthesia, 1839*

Louis Pasteur's theory of germs is ridiculous fiction.
    —*Pierre Pachet, professor of physiology, University of Toulouse, 1872*

There cannot always be fresh fields of conquest by the knife; there must be portions of the human frame that will ever remain sacred from its intrusions, at least in the surgeon's hands. That we have already, if not quite, reached these final limits, there can be little question. The abdomen, the chest, and the brain will be forever shut from the intrusion of the wise and humane surgeon.

—*Sir John Eric Ericksen, Surgeon-Extraordinary to Queen Victoria, 1873*

ELECTRICITY

. . . he who looks on the world with the eye of reverence must turn aside from this book as the result of an incurable delusion, whose sole effort is to detract from the dignity of nature.

—*a critic's reaction to George Simon Ohm's theory of electricity, 1827*

. . . a physicist who professed such heresies was unworthy to teach science.

—*unrecorded German minister of education, referring to Ohm*

There is no plea which will justify the use of high-tension and alternating currents, either in a scientific or a commercial sense. They are employed solely to reduce investment in copper wire and real estate. . . . My personal desire would be to prohibit entirely the use of alternating currents. They are as unnecessary as they are dangerous. . . . I can therefore see no justification for the introduction of a system which has no element of permanency and every element of danger to life and property. . . . I have always consistently opposed high-tension and alternating systems of electric lighting . . . not only on account of danger, but because of their general unreliability and unsuitability for any general system of distribution. . . .

The public may rest absolutely assured that safety will not be secured by burying these wires. The condensation of moisture, the ingress of water, the dissolving influence of coal gas and air-oxidation upon the various insulating compounds will result only in the transfer of deaths to man-holes, houses, stores, and offices, through the agency of the telephone, the low-pressure systems, and the apparatus of the high-tension current itself.

—*Thomas A. Edison,* 1889

Just as certain as death, [George] Westinghouse will kill a customer within six months after he puts in a system of any size.

—*Thomas A. Edison*

Thomas Edison's ideas of developing an incandescent lamp may be good enough for our transatlantic friends . . . but unworthy of the attention of practical or scientific men.

. . . I do not think there is the slightest chance of its [electricity] competing, in a general way, with gas. There are defects about the electric light which, unless some essential change takes place, must entirely prevent its application to ordinary lighting purposes.

. . . Without going into the consideration of many minor objections to the general adoption of such a [an electric] light on board ship, it may be sufficient to call attention to the following serious drawbacks, viz.: That whether fixed, revolving, or intermittent, a powerful light, such as is referred to, could not fail to interface very considerably with the distinctive arrangements for lighting the coasts by means of light-houses and light vessels. That such powerful lights would be almost certain to detract very much from the value of the smaller lights which the law compels all ships to show by night, and the risks of collision would be increased. That the glare of such powerful lights in crowded channels would be perplexing, and would probably cause such confusion that the risks of collision would be increased.

—*Select Committee on Lighting by Electricity,*
British House of Commons, 1879

COMMUNICATIONS

I watched his countenance closely, to see if he was not deranged . . . and I was assured by other senators after we left the room that they had no confidence in it.

> —*Senator Smith of Indiana after Samuel Morse demonstrated his telegraph, 1842*

. . . What was this telegraph to do? Would it transmit letters and newspapers? And besides, the telegraph might be made very mischievous, and secret information thereafter communicated to the prejudice of merchants.

> —*Senator George McDuffie, on an amendment to allocate funds to construct a telegraph line between Baltimore and New York City, 1845*

The operation of the telegraph between Washington and Baltimore had not satisfied [me] that under any rate of postage that could be adopted, its revenues could be made equal to its expenditures.

> —*Postmaster General Cave Johnson, when Samuel Morse tried to sell the rights to the telegraph to the U.S. Post Office (date unknown)*

. . . As far as I can judge, I do not look upon any system of wireless telegraphy as a serious competitor with our cables. Some years ago I said the same thing and nothing has since occurred to alter my views.

> —*Sir John Wolfe-Barry to stockholders of the Western Telegraph Company, 1907*

The wireless music box has no imaginable commercial value. Who would pay for a message sent to nobody in particular?

> —*associates of RCA chairman David Sarnoff, in response to his suggestion that the corporation invest in radio technology, circa 1920*

. . . You could put in this room, de Forest, all the radiotelephone apparatus that the country will ever need!

> —*W. W. Dean, president of the Dean Telephone Company, to Lee de Forest, inventor of the vacuum tube and "father" of television, 1907*

De Forest has said in many newspapers and over his signature that it would be possible to transmit human voice across the Atlantic before many years. Based on these absurd and deliberately misleading statements, the misguided public . . . has been persuaded to purchase stock in his company . . .

> —*Prosecutor in the 1913 stock fraud trial of Lee de Forest [De Forest was acquitted, but the judge advised him to get a "common garden variety of job and stick to it"]*

Well, then of what possible use can your "radiotelephone" be? It can't compare with the wire phone, you say, and it can't cover the distances that the wireless telegraph can cover. Then what the hell use is it anyway, Lee?

—unidentified friend of de Forest

THEORY OF EVOLUTION

My recent studies have made me more adverse than ever to the new scientific doctrines [Charles Darwin's theory of evolution] which are flourishing now in England. This sensational zeal reminds me of what I experienced as a young man in Germany, when the physio-philosophy of Oken had invaded every centre of scientific activity; and yet, what is there left of it? I trust to outlive this mania also.

—Louis Agassiz, circa 1870

All that was new in them was false, and all that was true in them was old.

—Professor Haughton of the University of Dublin, commenting on Darwin's findings, circa 1870

TRANSPORTATION

. . . the most ridiculous ideas have been formed, and circulated of their powers; and though I am of the opinion, when made the subject of attention amongst engineers, they will advance in improvement like other machines, they must as yet be considered only in their infancy, and as not having reached beyond the trammels of prejudice. It is far from my wish to promulgate to the world that the ridiculous expectations, or rather professions, of the enthusiastic speculist will be realised, and that we shall see them travelling at the rate of 12, 16, 18, or 20 miles an hour: nothing could do more harm towards their adoption, or general improvement, than the promulgation of such nonsense.

—Nicolas Wood, 1825

. . . that any general systems of conveying passengers would answer, to go at a velocity exceeding 10 miles an hour, or thereabouts, is extremely improbable.

—Thomas Tredgold, 1835

It was declared that its formation would prevent cows grazing and hens laying. The poisoned air from the locomotives would kill birds as they flew over them, and render the preservation of pheasants and foxes no longer possible. Householders adjoining the projected line were told that their houses would be burnt up by the fire thrown from the engine-chimneys, while the air around would be polluted by clouds of smoke. There would no longer be any use for horses; and if railways extended, the species would become extinguished, and oats and hay unsalable commodities. Traveling by road would be rendered highly dangerous, and country inns would be ruined. Boilers would burst and blow passengers to atoms. But there was always this consolation to wind up with—that the weight of the locomotive would completely prevent its moving, and that railways, even if made, could never be worked by steam-power!

—*pamphlets opposing the use of railroads in Britain,* 1823

I see what will be the effect of it; that it will set the whole world a-gadding. Twenty miles an hour, sir!—Why, you will not be able to keep an apprentice boy at his work! Every Saturday evening he must have a trip to Ohio to spend a Sunday with his sweetheart. Grave, plodding citizens will be flying about like comets. All local attachments will be at an end. It will encourage flightiness of intellect. Veracious people will turn into the most immeasurable liars. All conceptions will be exaggerated by the magnificent notions of distance.—Only a hundred miles off!—Tut, nonsense, I'll step across, madam, and bring your fan . . . And then, sir, there will be barrels of port, cargoes of flour, chaldrons of coal, and even lead and whiskey, and such like sober things that have always been used to slow travelling—whisking away like a sky rocket. It will upset all the gravity of the nation. . . . Upon the whole, sir, it is a pestilential, topsy-turvy, harum-scarum whirligig. Give me the old, solemn, straight forward, regular Dutch Canal—three miles an hour for expresses, and two rod jog-trot journeys—with a yoke of oxen for heavy loads. I go for beasts of burden. It is more formative and scriptural, and suits a moral and religious people better.—None of your hop skip and jump whimsies for me.

> —*article in* The Western Sun *of Vincennes, Indiana,* 1830

. . . a pretty plan; but there is just one point overlooked—that the steam engine requires a firm basis on which to work!

Sir Joseph Banks, explorer-naturalist and
president of the Royal Society, on applying
steam engines on ships, circa 1800

. . . even if the propeller had the power of propelling a vessel, it would be found altogether useless in practice, because the power being applied in the stern it would be absolutely impossible to make the vessel steer.

—Sir William Symonds, Surveyor of
the British Navy, on the idea of powering
a ship by means of a screw-propellor, 1837

Heavier-than-air flying machines are impossible.

—Lord Kelvin, president of the Royal Society, 1895

The actual building of roads devoted to motor cars is not for the near future, in spite of many rumors to that effect.

—article in Harper's Weekly, *1902*

Airplanes are interesting toys but of no military value.

—Ferdinand Foch, professor of strategy, French Army College, circa 1905 [Foch later became Allied Supreme Commander during World War One]

The Edison Company offered me the general superintendency of the company but only on condition that I would give up my gas engine and devote myself to something really useful.

—Henry Ford (in his memoirs)

WARFARE

The bow is a simple weapon; firearms are very complicated things
which get out of order in many ways . . . a very heavy weapon and
tires out soldiers on the march. Whereas also a bowman can let
off six aimed shots a minute, a musketeer can discharge but one in
two minutes.

*—Colonel Sir John Smyth opposing the change
from the longbow to musketry, 1591*

"What shall I do with the machine-guns today, sir?" would be
the question frequently asked by the officer in charge of a field
day. "Take the damn things to a flank and hide them!" was the
usual reply.

*—Brigadier-General Baker-Carr,
British Army, on the dislike of machine
guns by battalion commanders, 1914*

That Professor Goddard with his "chair" in Clark College and the countenancing of the Smithsonian Institution does not know the relation of action to reaction, and of the need to have something better than a vacuum against which to react—to say that would be absurd. Of course he only seems to lack the knowledge ladled out daily in high schools . . .

—*editorial in* The New York Times *on Robert Goddard, "father" of American rocket science, 1921*

I would much prefer to have Goddard interested in real scientific development than to have him primarily interested in more spectacular achievements which are of less real value

—*Charles A. Lindbergh, 1936*

The day of the battleship has not passed, and it is highly unlikely that an airplane, or fleet of them, could ever successfully sink a fleet of Navy vessels under battle conditions.

—*Franklin D. Roosevelt, Assistant Secretary of the Navy, 1922*

. . . As far as sinking a ship with a bomb is concerned, you just can't do it.

—U.S. Rear Admiral Clark Woodward, 1939

The editor of *Scientific American* wrote that this idea [a rocket-accelerated airplane bomb] was . . . too far-fetched to be considered.

—Willy Ley, astronautics expert, 1940

People have been talking about a 3,000-mile high-angle rocket shot from one continent to another, carrying an atomic bomb and so directed as to be a precise weapon. . . . I say, technically, I don't think anyone in the world knows how to do such a thing, and I feel confident that it will not be done for a very long period of time to come.

—Dr. Vannevar Bush on developing intercontinental missiles, 1945

Man will never reach the moon regardless of all future scientific advances.

—Lee de Forest, circa 1950

CANALS

All mankind has heard much of M. de Lesseps and his Suez Canal . . . I have a very strong opinion that such canal will not and cannot be made; that all the strength of the arguments adduced in the matter are hostile to it; and that steam navigation by land will and ought to be the means of transit through Egypt.

—Anthony Trollope on Ferdinand de Lesseps, designer of the Suez Canal, 1860

The Panama Canal is actually a thing of the past, and Nature in her works will soon obliterate all traces of French energy and money expended on the Isthmus.

—article in Scientific American, *1941*

ATOMIC ENERGY

I can accept the theory of relativity as little as I can accept the existence of atoms and other such dogma.

—Ernst Mach, circa 1930

The energy produced by the breaking down of the atom is a very poor kind of thing. Anyone who looks for a source of power in the transformation of the atom is talking moonshine.

—Sir Ernest Rutherford, 1933

Atomic energy might be as good as our present-day explosives, but it is unlikely to produce anything very much more dangerous.

—Sir Winston Churchill, 1939

That is the biggest fool thing we have ever done. . . . The bomb will never go off, and I speak as an expert in explosives.
> —*Admiral William Leahy to President Harry S.*
> *Truman regarding the atomic bomb, 1945*

COMPUTERS

I think there is a world market for maybe five computers.
> —*Thomas Watson, chairman of the board, IBM, 1943*

Computers in the future may weigh no more than 1.5 tons.
> —Popular Mechanics, *1949*

I have traveled the length and breadth of this country and talked with the best people, and I can assure you that data processing is a fad that won't last out the year.

—editor of business books, Prentice Hall publishers, 1957

But what . . . is it [a microchip] good for?

—engineer at the Advanced Computing Systems Division of IBM, 1968

There is no reason anyone would want a computer in their home.

—Ken Olson, founder of Digital Equipment Corp., 1972

We went to Atari and said, "Hey, we've got this amazing thing, even built with some of your parts, and what do you think about funding us?" They said, "No." So then we went to Hewlett-Packard, and they said, "We don't need you. You haven't got through college yet."
— *Apple Computer, Inc. founder Steve Jobs, on attempts to interest the two corporations in a personal computer that he and Steve Wozniak had developed*

"640K" ought to be enough [computer memory] for anybody.
— *Bill Gates, Microsoft founder, 1981*

One hundred million dollars is way too much to pay for Microsoft.
— *unidentified IBM executive, 1982*

OTHER INVENTIONS AND BUSINESS

The trade of Advertising is now so near to perfection that it is not easy to propose any improvement.

—The Idler, *1759*

[They] might as well try to light London with a slice from the moon.
—*William H. Wollaston, English chemist, commenting on a proposal to light British cities with gas lamps, circa 1800*

Drill for oil? You mean drill into the ground to try and find oil? You're crazy.
—*workers whom Edwin L. Drake tried to hire on his project to drill for oil in Titusville, Pennsylvania, 1859*

Stocks have reached what looks like a permanently high plateau.
   —*Irving Fisher, professor of economics, Yale University, 1929*

The concept is interesting and well formed, but in order to earn better than a "C," the idea must be feasible.
   —*a professor of management at Yale University, commenting on the term paper by Fred Smith (which earned a "C") that outlined a plan for a reliable overnight delivery service; Smith went on to found Federal Express in 1973*

A cookie store is a bad idea. Besides, the market research reports say America likes crispy cookies, not soft and chewy cookies like you make.
   —*unidentified response to Debbi Fields's plan to start Mrs. Fields Cookies*

If I had thought about it, I wouldn't have done the experiment. The literature was full of examples that said you can't do this.
—Spencer Silver on the work that led to the adhesives for 3M Post-It notepads

⁓

You want to have consistent and uniform muscle development across all of your muscles? It can't be done. It's just a fact of life. You just have to accept inconsistent muscle development as an unalterable condition of weight training.
—response to Arthur Jones, who went on to invent Nautilus fitness machines.

⁓

. . . The advancement of the arts from year to year taxes our credulity and seems to presage the arrival of that period when further improvements must end.
—Henry L. Ellsworth, commissioner, U.S. Office of Patents, 1844

⁓

Everything that can be invented has been invented.
  —*Charles H. Duell, commissioner, U.S. Office of Patents,* 1899

This company is not bust. We are merely in a cyclical decline.
              —*Lord Stokes, chairman of British Leyland,* 1974

We've got to pause and ask ourselves: How much clean air do
we need?

                    —*Lee Iacocca, former chairman,*
                                 Ford Motor Company

I tell you, it's Big Business. If there's one word to describe Atlantic City, it's Big Business. Or two words—Big Business.
   —*Donald Trump, as quoted in a 1989* Time *magazine article*

⁓

You can't just let nature run wild!
   —*Walter Hickel, governor of Alaska, on a plan to kill wolves*

⁓

If you set aside Three Mile Island and Chernobyl, the safety record of nuclear energy is really very good.
                    —*Paul O'Neill, secretary of the Treasury*

⁓

IV.

THE
MEDIA

Newspapers, Magazines, Radio, TV, and the Movies

At the present moment, the whole fleet is lit up. When I say "lit up," I mean lit up by fairy lamps. It's fantastic. It isn't a fleet at all. It's just . . . It's fairyland. The whole fleet is in fairyland. Now, if you'll follow me through . . . the next few moments you'll find the fleet doing odd things.

> —*Lieutenant Commander Tommy Woodroofe describing the "illumination" of the Royal Navy fleet at Spithead, 1937 (it seems the commentator was also well lit up)*

I think I know that one. Is it Jewish?

> —*quiz show contestant when asked for the Pope's religion*

If it weren't for electricity, we'd all be watching television by candlelight.

> —*George Gobel, television personality*

Shergar.
> —*contestant on the television quiz show,* The Weakest Link, *when asked which famous racehorse's name was the word "murder" spelled backwards*

A memorial has been set up for the victims of the atrocity outside the west door of Westminster Abbey.
> —*BBC broadcast*

The U.S. may increase aid to the former Soviet Union by as much as a billion dollars to help stabilize the rubble.
> —*radio news report confusing ruble with "rubble"*

The telephone company is urging people not to use the telephone unless it is absolutely necessary, in order to keep the lines open for emergency calls. We'll be right back after this break to give away a pair of Phil Collins concert tickets to caller number 95.

—unidentified radio disc jockey after the 1990 Los Angeles earthquake

That's Paris, Ontario, not Paris, Italy.

—host of a Canadian children's television show

Rotarians, be patriotic! Learn to shoot yourself.

—Chicago Rotary Club journal, Gyrator

The crime bill passed by the senate would reinstate the federal
death penalty for certain violent crimes: assassinating the President;
hijacking an airliner; and murdering a government poultry inspector.
—*Knight Ridder News Service dispatch*

The farmers in Annapolis Valley are pleased to announce that this
year there will be an abundance of apples. This is particularly good
news because most of the farmers haven't had a good crap in years.
—*unidentified Maryland television news broadcaster*

Ladies and gentlemen . . . and now Mr. Eddie Playbody will pee
for you.
—*radio announcer introducing banjoist, Eddie Peabody*

An end is in sight to the severe weather shortage.

—*Ian Macaskill, BBC weather*

Sir Stifford Craps.

—*Lowell Thomas, radio commentator, presenting the British prime minister, Sir Stafford Cripps*

The Duck and Doochess of Windsor.

—*unidentified radio announcer referring to the Duke and Duchess of Windsor*

Tuesday Night at the Movies will be seen on Saturday this week instead of Monday.

—unidentified television announcer

Red squirrels . . . you don't see many of them since they became extinct.

—Michael Aspel on British Radio 2

Well, here it is Christmas. So we have a skeleton screw, er, skeleton crew here today.

—unidentified Minnesota radio announcer

Retraction: The "Greek Special" is a huge, 18-inch pizza and not a huge, 18-inch penis, as described in an ad. Blondie's Pizza would like to apologize for any confusion Friday's ad may have caused.

—correction in The Daily Californian

. . . and from Washington comes word that President and Mrs. Lincoln will spend Nixon's birthday at Key Biscayne, Florida, on February twelfth.

—unidentified radio newscaster

As a prize—a beautiful riding mower with optional ass scratcher!

—announcer on television show,
who meant to say "grass catcher"

We now will hear "Deck Your Balls with Halls of Helly" . . . "Deck
your Bell with Balls of Holly" . . . er . . . a Christmas selection.
—BBC radio announcer

Then you add two forkfuls of cooking oil . . .
—recipe given on television's The French Chef

Ladies and gentlemen, now you can have a bikini for a ridiculous
figure.
—unidentified radio announcer

Be with us again next Saturday at 10 P.M. for "High Fidelity,"
designed to help music lovers increase their reproduction.
—unidentified radio announcer

When you are thirsty, try 7 UP the refreshing drink in the green bottle with the big 7 on it and u-p after.

—unidentified radio announcer

Ask us about our cup size or our favorite position, but—please—no personal questions.

—twin models, when asked who was older

I don't diet. I just don't eat as much as I'd like to.

—Linda Evangelista, model

It's just my same normal life, but now I get to go to movie premieres and to parties.

—Bridget Hall, model

～

To say this book is about me (which is the main reason I was uncomfortable—me, me, me, me, me . . . frightening!) is ridiculous. This book is not about me.

—Kate Moss, model/actress, on her book,
Kate: The Kate Moss Book

～

Smoking kills. If you're killed, you've lost a very important part of your life.

—Brooke Shields, actress/model, during an
interview to front an anti-smoking campaign

～

I believe that mink are raised for being turned into fur coats and if we didn't wear fur coats, those little animals would never have been born. So is it better not to have been born, or to have lived for one or two years to have been turned into a fur coat? I don't know.

—*Barbi Benton, model and actress*

It's not listed in the Bible, but my spiritual gift, my specific calling from God, is to be a television talk show host.

—*James Bakker, televangelist*

Please accept my resignation. I don't care to belong to any club that will have me as a member.

—*Groucho Marx, in a letter written to the owner of a Hollywood club*

I would not live forever, because we should not live forever, because if we were supposed to live forever, then we would live forever, but we cannot live forever, which is why I would not live forever.

—Miss Alabama, in the 1994 Miss USA contest, responding to the question "If you could live forever, would you, and why?"

Whenever I watch TV and see those poor starving kids all over the world, I can't help but cry. I mean, I'd love to be skinny like that, but not with all those flies and death and stuff.

—Mariah Carey, singer

I don't feel we did wrong in taking this great country away from them. There were great numbers of people who needed new land, and the Indians were selfishly trying to keep it for themselves.

—John Wayne

Who the hell wants to hear actors talk?
            *—Harry Warner of Warner Brothers movie
            studio, when asked about sound in films*

TV won't be able to hold any market after the first six months.
People will soon get tired of staring at a plywood box every night.
            *—Darryl Zanuck, head of 20th
            Century Fox movie studios, 1946*

Movies are a fad. Audiences really want to see live actors on a stage.
            —Charlie Chaplin

I'm just glad it'll be Clark Gable who's falling on his face, and not Gary Cooper.

> —*Gary Cooper, on his decision not to take the leading role in* Gone With The Wind

As a mother, I know that homosexuals cannot biologically reproduce children; therefore, they must recruit our children.

> —*Anita Bryant*

The government is not doing enough about cleaning up the environment. This is a good planet.

> —*Mr. New Jersey contestant, when asked what he would do with a million dollars*

Rock 'n' roll is phony and false, and sung, written, and played for the most part by cretinous goons.

—*Frank Sinatra, 1957*

We don't like their sound, and guitar music is on the way out.

—*Decca Recording Company executive,*
turning down the Beatles, 1962

HALL OF SHAME MEMBER #11

The king of all entertainment malapropisms was Samuel Goldwyn, the producer of such films as Pride Of The Yankees, The Best Years Of Our Lives, *and* Guys And Dolls *(the "G" in "MGM" stands for Goldwyn). Among his legendary Goldwynisms were:*

Spare no expense to make everything as economical as possible.

Gentlemen, include me out.

We can get all the Indians we need at the reservoir.

Anything that man says, you've got to take with a dose of salts.

Why did you do that? Every Tom, Dick and Harry is named Sam!
— when a friend told him he named his son Sam

True, I've been a long time making up my mind, but now I'm giving you a definite answer. I won't say yes, and I won't say no—but I'm giving you a definite maybe.

A verbal agreement isn't worth the paper it's written on.

If you won't give me your word of honor, will you give me your promise?

All right, where they got lesbians, we'll use Austrians.
> —*when told that he couldn't make a movie because the script contained references to lesbians*

Television has raised writing to a new low.

Never make forecasts, especially about the future.

Go see that turkey for yourself, and see for yourself why you shouldn't see it.

I'm willing to admit that I may not always be right, but I am never wrong.

If I could drop dead right now, I'd be the happiest man alive.

NEWSPAPER HEADLINES

∽ Dewey Defeats Truman
> —Chicago Daily Tribune *headline the morning after*
> *Harry S. Truman's 1948 presidential victory*

∽ Police Suspicious After Body Found in Graveyard

∽ Male Infertility Can Be Passed on to Children

∽ Statistics Show that Mortality Increases Perceptibly in the Military During Wartime

∽ Include Your Children When Baking Cookies

∽ Something Went Wrong in Jet Crash, Experts Say

∽ Police Begin Campaign to Run Down Jaywalkers

∽ Drunks Get Nine Months in Violin Case

∽ Iraqi Head Seeks Arms

∽ Prostitutes Appeal to Pope

∽ Panda Mating Fails; Veterinarian Takes Over

∽ British Left Waffles on Falkland Islands

෬ Clinton Wins Budget; More Lies Ahead

෬ Plane Too Close to Ground, Crash Probe Told

෬ Miners Refuse to Work After Death

෬ Juvenile Court to Try Shooting Defendant

෬ Stolen Painting Found by Tree

෬ Two Sisters Reunited After 18 Years in Checkout Counter

෬ War Dims Hope for Peace

- Couple Slain; Police Suspect Homicide

- Man Struck by Lightning Faces Battery Charge

- New Study of Obesity Looks for Larger Test Group

- Astronaut Takes Blame for Gas in Space

- Kids Make Nutritious Snacks

- Local High School Dropouts Cut in Half

- Typhoon Rips through Cemetery; Hundreds Dead

↪ Deaf Mute Gets New Hearing in Killing

↪ House Passes Gas Tax on to Senate

↪ Stiff Opposition Expected to Casketless Funeral Plan

↪ Two Convicts Evade Noose, Jury Hung

↪ William Kelly Was Fed Secretary

↪ Milk Drinkers Are Turning to Powder

↪ Safety Experts Say School Bus Passengers Should Be Belted

∽ Quarter of a Million Chinese Live on Water

∽ Farmer Bill Dies in House

∽ Queen Mary Having Bottom Scraped

∽ NJ Judge to Rule on Nude Beach

∽ Child's Stool Great for Use in Garden

∽ Dr. Ruth to Talk about Sex with Newspaper Editors

∽ Soviet Virgin Lands Short of Goal Again

∾ Eye Drops Off Shelf

∾ Squad Helps Dog Bite Victim

∾ Dealers Will Hear Car Talk at Noon

∾ Enraged Cow Injures Farmer with Ax

∾ Lawmen from Mexico Barbecue Guests

∾ Illiterate? Write Today for Free Help

∾ Never Withhold Herpes from Loved One

෴ Drunk Drivers Paid $1,000 in 1984

෴ Autos Killing 110 a Day; Let's Resolve to Do Better

෴ If Strike Isn't Settled Quickly It May Last a While

෴ Smokers Are Productive, But Death Cuts Efficiency

෴ Cold Wave Linked to Temperatures

෴ Child's Death Ruins Couple's Holiday

෴ Blind Woman Gets New Kidney from Dad She Hasn't Seen
  in Years

᠁ Death Causes Loneliness, Feeling of Isolation

᠁ Whatever Their Motives, Moms Who Kill Kids Still
Shock Us

᠁ Survey Finds Dirtier Subways After Cleaning Jobs Were Cut

᠁ Larger Kangaroos Leap Farther, Researchers Find

᠁ "Light" Meals Are Lower in Fat, Calories

᠁ Alcohol Ads Promote Drinking

᠁ Malls Try to Attract Shoppers

⌒ Low Wages Said Key to Poverty

⌒ Man Shoots Neighbor With Machete

⌒ Tomatoes Come in Big, Little, Medium Sizes

⌒ Dirty-Air Cities Far Deadlier than Clean Ones, Study Shows

⌒ Man Run Over by Freight Train Dies

⌒ Scientists See Quakes in LA Future

⌒ Wachtler Tells Graduates that Life in Jail Is Demeaning

꙯ Prosecution Paints O.J. as a Wife-Killer

꙯ Economist Uses Theory to Explain Economy

꙯ Bible Church's Focus Is the Bible

꙯ Clinton Pledges Restraint in Use of Nuclear Weapons

꙯ Discoveries: Older Blacks Have Edge in Longevity

꙯ Court Rules Boxer Shorts Are Indeed Underwear

꙯ Biting Nails Can Be Sign of Tenseness in a Person

◌ How We Feel About Ourselves Is the Core of Self-Esteem

◌ Fish Lurk in Streams

◌ Lawyer Says Client Is Not That Guilty

◌ Alzheimer's Center Prepares for an Affair to Remember

NEWSPAPER CLASSIFIED ADS

◦ One man, seven woman hot tub — $850/Offer.

◦ Amana washer $100. Owned by clean bachelor who seldom washed.

◦ Snowblower for sale . . . only used on snowy days.

◦ Free puppies . . . part German shepherd/part dog.

◦ Two wire-mesh butchering gloves, one 5-finger, one 3-finger; pair: $15.

↫ Cows, calves never bred . . . also 1 gay bull for sale.

↫ Free puppies: 1/2 cocker spaniel—1/2 sneaky neighbor's dog.

↫ Free Yorkshire terrier: 8 Years Old. Unpleasant Little Dog.

↫ Full-sized mattress: 20-year warranty. Like new. Slight urine smell.

↫ Free: 1 can of pork & beans with purchase of 3 Br 2 Bth Home.

↫ Bill's Septic Cleaning—"We haul American-made products."

- Found: dirty white dog . . . looks like a rat . . . been out awhile . . . better be reward.

- Get a Little John: The Traveling Urinal—holds 2½ bottles of beer.

- Georgia Peaches—California Grown—89 Cents Lb.

- Nice parachute—never opened—used once—slightly stained.

- Free: farm kittens. Ready to eat.

- American flag—60 stars—pole included—$100.

∽ Notice: To person or persons who took the large pumpkin on Highway 87 near Southridge Storage. Please return the pumkin and be checked. Pumpkin may be radioactive. All other plants in vicinity are dead.

∽ Our sofa seats the whole mob—and it's made of 100% Italian leather.

∽ Joining nudist colony, must sell washer & dryer—$300.

∽ Open House—Body Shapers Toning Salon—Free Coffee & Donuts.

∽ Fully cooked boneless smoked man—$2.09 Lb.

↷ Dinner Special—Turkey $2.35; Chicken or Beef $2.25; Children $2.00.

↷ For sale: an antique desk suitable for lady with thick legs and large drawers.

↷ For sale: a quilted high chair that can be made into a table, potty-chair, rocking horse, refrigerator, spring coat, size 8 and fur collar.

↷ Now is your chance to have your ears pierced and get an extra pair to take home, too.

↷ Wanted: 50 girls for stripping machine operators in factory.

∽ No matter what your topcoat is made of, this miracle spray will make it really repellent.

∽ Seven ounces of choice sirloin steak, boiled to your likeness and smothered with golden fried onion rings.

∽ Tired of cleaning yourself? Let me do it.

∽ Twenty dozen bottles of excellent Old Tawny Port, sold to pay for charges, the owner having lost sight of, and bottled by us last year.

∽ Dog for sale: eats anything and is fond of children.

∽ Vacation Special: have your home exterminated.

- The hotel has bowling alleys, tennis courts, comfortable beds, and other athletic facilities.

- Get rid of aunts: Zap does the job in 24 hours.

- Toaster: A gift that every member of the family appreciates. Automatically burns toast.

- Sheer stockings: Designed for fancy dress, but so serviceable that lots of women wear nothing else.

- Stock up and save. Limit: one.

- Save regularly in our bank. You'll never regret it. We build bodies that last a lifetime.

○ This is the model home for your future. It was panned by *Better Homes and Gardens*.

○ For rent: 6-room hated apartment.

○ Man, honest. Will take anything.

○ Wanted: chambermaid in rectory. Love in, $200 a month. References required.

○ Wanted: Part-time married girls for soda fountain in sandwich shop.

◦ Man wanted to work in dynamite factory. Must be willing to travel.

◦ Used cars: Why go elsewhere to be cheated? Come here first!

◦ Christmas tag sale: handmade gifts for the hard-to-find person.

◦ Modular sofas: only $299. For rest or fore play.

◦ Wanted: Hair-cutter. Excellent growth potential.

◦ Wanted: Man to take care of cow that does not smoke or drink.

᧞ Our experienced Mom will care for your child. Fenced yard, meals, and smacks included.

᧞ Auto Repair Service: Free pick-up and delivery. Try us once, you'll never go anywhere again.

᧞ See ladies blouses. 50% off!

᧞ Holcross pullets. Starting to lay Betty Clayton.

᧞ Wanted: Preparer of food. Must be dependable, like the food business, and be willing to get hands dirty.

↷ Wanted: Widower with school-age children requires person to assume general housekeeping duties. Must be capable of contributing to growth of family.

↷ Mixing bowl set designed to please a cook with round bottom for efficient beating.

↷ Mother's helper—peasant working conditions.

↷ Semi-Annual After-Christmas Sale.

↷ And now, the Superstore—unequaled in size, unmatched in variety, unrivaled inconvenience.

V

LANGUAGE

Malapropisms:

Mrs. Malaprop (her name means "inappropriate") was a character in Richard Sheridan's 1775 play, The Rivals. *She has lent her name to the variety of verbal miscues she came out with, such as:*

- "Forget this fellow—to *illiterate* him, I say, quite from your memory.
  [obliterate]

- "Oh! it gives me the *hydrostatics* to such a degree."
  [hysterics]

- "I hope you will represent her to the captain as an object not altogether *illegible.*"
  [eligible]

❧ " . . . she might *reprehend* the true meaning of what she is saying."
[comprehend]

❧ "I am sorry to say, Sir Anthony, that my *affluence* over my niece is very small."
[influence]

❧ "Why, murder's the matter! slaughter's the matter! killing's the matter!—but he can tell you the *perpendiculars*."
[particulars]

❧ "His *physiognomy* is so grammatical!"
[phraseology]

❧ "I am sure I have done everything in my power since I *exploded* the affair."
[exposed]

‍ "... if ever you betray what you are entrusted with ... you forfeit my *malevolence* for ever ..."
[benevolence]

‍ "Sure, if I *reprehend* any thing in this world, it is the use of my *oracular* tongue, and a nice *derangement* of *epitaphs!*"
[apprehend, vernacular, arrangement, epithets]

‍ "She's as headstrong as an *allegory* on the banks of the Nile."
[alligator]

MALAPROPS FROM GRADE SCHOOL, HIGH SCHOOL, AND COLLEGE EXAMINATIONS

➭ Samuel Morse invented a code for telepathy.

➭ Louis Pasteur discovered a cure for rabbis.

➭ In the Renaissance, Martin Luther was nailed to the church door at Wittenberg for selling papal indulgences. He died a horrible death, being excommunicated by a bull.

➭ The walls of Notre Dame Cathedral are supported by flying buttocks.

➭ The painter Donatello's interest in the female nude made him the father of the Renaissance.

↷ Gutenberg invented the Bible.

↷ Sir Frances Drake circumcised the world with a 100-foot clipper.

↷ Johann Sebastian Bach wrote a great many musical compositions and had a large number of children. In between he practiced on the old spinster which he kept up in his attic.

↷ Bach was the most famous composer in the world and so was Handel. Handel was half German, half Italian, and half English.

↷ Pharaoh forced the Hebrew slaves to make bread without straw.

↷ Moses led them to the Red Sea, where they made unleavened bread, which is bread made without any ingredients.

○ Afterwards, Moses went up on Mount Cyanide to get the Ten Commandments.

○ Solomon, one of David's sons, had 500 wives and 500 porcupines.

○ In the Olympic Games, Greeks ran races, jumped, hurled the biscuits, and threw the java. The reward to the victor was a coral wreath.

○ The government of Athens was democratic because the people took the law into their own hands.

○ There were no wars in Greece, as the mountains were so high that they couldn't climb over to see what their neighbors were doing.

○ People have sex, while nouns have genders.

- Christmas is a time for happiness for every child, adult, and adulteress.

- Women like to do things in circles, where they sew, talk, and do their meddling.

- Good punctuation means not to be late.

- The American colonists won the Revolutionary War and no longer had to pay for taxis.

- "Don't" is a contraption.

- Italics are what Italians write in.

∽ Most words are easy to spell once you get the letters write.

∽ Protons are found in both meat and electricity.

∽ The air is thin high up in the sky; down here, it's fat.

∽ Adam and Eve wore nothing but figments.

∽ Antarctica is like the regular Arctic, but ritzier.

∽ Abraham Lincoln became America's greatest Precedent.

∽ The bowels are a,e,i,o,u, and sometimes y.

∽ Guests at Roman banquets wore garlics in their hair.

∽ He worked in the government as a civil serpent.

∽ When a baby is born, the doctor cuts its biblical chord.

∽ The flood damage was so bad they had to evaporate the city.

∽ Flying saucers are just an optical conclusion.

∽ Homer wrote *The Oddity*. [*The Odyssey*]

∽ A horse divided against itself cannot stand.

∽ The bride walked down the isle.

◦ Deader than a hangnail.

◦ Charles Darwin wrote *The Organ of the Species*. [*The Origin of Species*]

◦ She was as mad as a wet blanket.

◦ You purify water by filtering it and then forcing it through an aviator.

◦ Everything's fine—just honky-tonky.

◦ The climate of the Sarah Desert is so hot that certain areas are cultivated by irritation.

꙾ The U.S. Constitution was adopted to secure domestic hostility.

꙾ Columbus discovered America while cursing about the Atlantic.

꙾ The doctor felt the man's purse and said there was no hope.

꙾ Damp weather is very hard on the sciences.

꙾ The government of England is a limited mockery.

꙾ Let dead dogs sleep.

꙾ Gravity was invented by Isaac Walton.

∽ Greeks invented three kinds of columns: Corinthian, Doric, and Ironic.

∽ Growing up the trellis were pink and yellow concubines.

∽ Henry VIII found walking difficult because he had an abbess on his knee.

∽ If a pronoun is a word used in place of a noun, a proverb is a pronoun used in place of a verb.

∽ I'm not the kind of person who wears his heart up his sleeve.

∽ King Alfred conquered the Dames.

∽ People who live in Moscow are called Mosquitoes.

∽ Never look a gift horse in the mouse.

∽ All that glitters is not cold.

∽ The squaws carried porpoises on their back.

∽ Most people in the Middle Ages were alliterate.

∽ Salmon swim upstream to spoon.

∽ Brigham Young led the Morons to Utah.

༆ The first book of the Bible is the book of Guinesses.

༆ In the Olympic Games, Greeks hurled the biscuits.

༆ Wat Tyler led the Pheasants' Revolt.

༆ The patient had a deviant septum.

༆ In the Bible, Jacob stole his brother Esau's birthmark.

༆ Socrates died from taking a poison called wedlock.

༆ Julius Caesar extinguished himself on the battlefields of Gaul.

◌ Marriage to one wife is called monotony.

◌ Rome wasn't burned in a day.

◌ He always puts his foot in his soup.

◌ King Harold mustard his troops before the Battle of Hastings.

◌ The police surrounded the building and threw an accordion around the block.

◌ He was between a rock and the deep blue sea.

◌ The mountain range between France and Spain is the Pyramids.

◡ A leopard is a form of dotted lion.

◡ Money roots out all evil.

◡ Let sleeping ducks lie.

◡ Let's get down to brass roots.

◡ Achilles' mother dipped him in the River Stinks until he became immortal.

◡ The people who followed Jesus were called the Twelve Opossums.

◡ The Greeks gave winning athletes a coral reef.

- A rolling stone gathers no moths.

- The battle was won due to gorilla warfare.

- The liquid rose because of caterpillar action.

- To prevent head colds, use an agonizer to spray medicine into your nose.

- Don't bite the hand that lays the golden egg.

- The Second Amendment gives citizens the right to bare arms.

- The store was closed for altercations.

෴ It is beyond my apprehension.

෴ Listen to the blabbing brook.

෴ He's a tough and remorseful guy.

෴ We seem to have unleased a hornet's nest.

෴ Be sure and put some of those neutrons on my salad.

෴ My new coat has lots of installation.

෴ The amount of education you have determines your roll in life.

FROM HIGH SCHOOL AND COLLEGE EXAMINATIONS IN THE SUBJECTS OF MUSIC APPRECIATION AND MUSIC HISTORY

- The principal singer of nineteenth-century opera was called the pre-Madonna.

- It is easy to teach anyone to play the maracas. Just grip the neck and shake him in rhythm.

- Gregorian chant has no music, just singers singing the same lines.

- Sherbet composed the Unfinished Symphony.

- All female parts were sung by castrati. We don't know exactly what they sounded like because they had no descendants.

෨ Music sung by two people at the same time is called a duel.

෨ If they sing without music it is called Acapulco.

෨ A virtuoso is a musician with real high morals.

෨ Contralto is a low sort of music that only ladies sing.

෨ Diatonic is a low-calorie soda.

෨ A fugue was something the Hatfields and the McCoys had.

෨ A harp is a nude piano.

꙳ The main trouble with a French horn is that it is too tangled up.

꙳ An interval in music is the distance from one piano to the next.

꙳ The correct way to find the key to a piece of music is to use a pitchfork.

꙳ Agitato is a state of mind when one's finger slips in the middle of playing a piece.

꙳ Refrain means don't do it. A refrain in music is the part you'd better not try to sing.

꙳ Most authorities agree that music of antiquity was written long ago.

꙳ My favorite composer was Opus.

꙾ Agnus Dei was a woman composer famous for her church music.

꙾ Henry Purcell was a well-known composer few people have ever heard of.

꙾ An opera is a big song.

꙾ When a singer sings, he stirs up the air and makes it hit any passing eardrums. But if he is good, he knows how to keep it from hurting.

꙾ A good orchestra is always ready to play if the conductor steps on the podium.

꙾ Morris dancing is a country survival from times when people were happy.

⌒ A tuba is much larger than its name.

⌒ Instruments come in many shapes, sizes, and orchestras.

⌒ Q: What are kettle drums called? A: Kettle drums.

⌒ Q: What are kettle drums called? A: Another name for kettle drums is timpani. But I think I will stick with the first name and learn it good.

⌒ A trumpet is an instrument when it is not an elephant sound.

⌒ While trombones have tubes, trumpets prefer to wear valves.

⌒ The double bass is also called the bass viol, string bass, and bass fiddle. It has so many names because it is so huge.

◦ When electric currents go through them, guitars start making sounds. So would anybody.

◦ Cymbals are round, metal clangs.

◦ A bassoon looks like nothing I have ever heard.

◦ Last month I found out how a clarinet works by taking it apart. I both found out and got in trouble.

◦ Q: Is the saxophone a brass or woodwind instrument? A: Yes.

◦ The concertmaster of an orchestra is always the person who sits in the first chair of the first violins. This means that when a person is elected concertmaster, he has to hurry up and learn how to play a violin real good.

○ For some reason, they always put a treble clef in front of every line of flute music. You just watch.

○ I can't reach the brakes on this piano!

○ Anyone who can read all the instrument notes at the same time gets to be the conductor.

○ Instrumentalist is a many-purpose word for many player-types.

○ The flute is the skinny-high shaped-sounded instrument.

○ The most dangerous part about playing cymbals is near the nose.

○ A contra-bassoon is like a bassoon, only more so.

◈ Tubas are a bit too much.

◈ "Music instrument" has a plural called "orchestra."

◈ Just about any animal skin can be stretched over a frame to make a pleasant sound once the animal is removed.

⌒

And among musical compositions that have been cited:

◈ Bronze Lullaby

◈ Taco Bell Cannon

◈ Beethoven's Erotica

↩ Tchaikovsky's Cracknutter Sweet

↩ Gershwin's Rap City in Blue

OTHER LINGUISTIC LEAPFROGS

↩ Abraham Lincoln wrote the Gettysburg Address while traveling from Washington to Gettysburg on the back of an envelope.

↩ You have to take the bad with the worse.

↩ *The Iliad* of Homer was not written by Homer, but by another man of that name.

⌒ Although the patient had never been fatally ill before, he woke up dead.

⌒ William Tell shot an arrow through an apple while standing on his son's head.

⌒ At least half their customers who fly to New York come by plane.

⌒ Before I start speaking, I'd like to say something.

⌒ The blood circulates through the body by flowing down one leg and up the other.

⌒ The book was so exciting I couldn't finish it until I put it down.

↪ Congressman Smith stayed after the town meeting and discussed the high cost of living with several women.

↪ The conviction carries a penalty of one to ten years in Alabama.

↪ The difference between a king and a president is that a king is the son of his father and a president isn't.

↪ During the Napoleonic Wars the crowned heads of Europe were trembling in their shoes.

↪ Every silver lining has a cloud around it.

↪ Female moths are called myths.

꙾ Fine furniture at reasonable prices: antique, colonial, and temporary.

꙾ The four seasons are salt, pepper, mustard, and vinegar.

꙾ George Washington married Martha Curtis and in due time became the father of his country.

꙾ The Gorgons had long snakes in their hair. They looked like women, only more horrible.

꙾ Athens was a democracy because people took the law into their own hands.

꙾ Napoleon wanted an heir to inherit his power, but since Josephine was a baroness, she couldn't bear children.

↪ It's time to grab the bull by the tail and look it in the eye.

↪ The jury's verdict showed they were of one mind: temporarily insane.

↪ Lincoln's mother died in infancy, and he was born in a log cabin which he built with his own hands.

↪ Magna Carta provided that no free men should be hanged twice for the same offense.

↪ The match was so close that it was hanging on a cliff the whole time.

↪ Most of the houses in France are made of plaster of Paris.

⤙ The car had no damage whatsoever in the accident, and the other car had even less.

⤙ One by-product of raising cattle is calves.

⤙ You have to say about him, he doesn't mince his punches.

⤙ The sacred cows have come home to roost.

⤙ She held out her hand. The young man took it and left.

⤙ The spinal column is a long bunch of bones. Your head sits on the top, and you sit on the bottom.

- That snake in the grass is barking up the wrong tree.

- He saw three other people in the restaurant, and half of those were waiters.

- These hemorrhoids are a pain in the neck.

- A virgin forest is a forest where the hand of man has never set foot.

- When they fought with the Persians, the Greeks were outnumbered because the Persians had more men.

SPOONERISMS

The Rev. W. A. Spooner (1844—1930) was prone to transposing initial letters or syllables, such as "It is kisstomary to cuss the bride" instead of ". . . customary to kiss the bride." Like Mrs. Malaprop, he committed such slips of the tongue as:

- fighting a liar [lighting a fire]

- you hissed my mystery lecture [you missed my history lecture]

- searched every crook and nanny [searched every nook and cranny]

⤷ cattle ships and bruisers [battleships and cruisers]

⤷ nosy little crook [cozy little nook]

⤷ a blushing crow [a crushing blow]

⤷ kinquering congs their titles take [conquering kings their titles take] (a hymn)

⤷ I see before me tons of soil [sons of toil]

⤷ We all know what it is to have a half-warmed fish inside us [half-formed wish]

↪ let us drink to the queer old Dean [let us drink to the dear old Queen]

↪ we'll have the hags flung out [we'll have the flags hung out]

↪ you've tasted two worms [you've wasted two terms]

↪ our shoving leopard [our loving shepherd]

↪ is the bean dizzy? [is the Dean busy?]

Mondegreens

Someone misheard the lyrics to a Scottish ballad, "The Bonnie Earl of Morey," and instead of "Ye Highlands and ye lowlands/Oh, where hae ye been?/They have slain the Earl of Morey/And laid him on the green," the person heard " . . . and lady Mondegreen."

That's how misheard lyrics and lines of poetry have come to be called Mondegreens.

"Gladly, the cross-eyed bear."

> —*the hymn,* Gladly The Cross I'd Bear

"Sleep in heavenly peas."

> —*the Christmas carol,* Silent Night:
> *"Sleep in heavenly peace."*

"There's a bathroom on the right."
>> —*Creedence Clearwater Revival, Bad Moon Rising:*
>>> *"There's a bad moon on the rise."*

"Excuse me while I kiss this guy."
>> —*Jimi Hendrix, Purple Haze:*
>> *"Excuse me while I kiss the sky."*

"Dead ants are my friends; they're blowin' in the wind."
>> —*Bob Dylan, Blowin' in the Wind:*
>> *"The answer my friend is blowin' in the wind."*

"Midnight after you're wasted."
—*Maria Muldaur, Midnight at the Oasis:*
"Midnight at the oasis"

"The girl with colitis goes by."
—*The Beatles, Lucy in the Sky with Diamonds:*
"The girl with kaleidoscope eyes."

"She's got a chicken to ride."
—*The Beatles, Ticket to Ride:*
"She's got a ticket to ride."

"Sunday monkey won't play piano song, play piano song."

—*The Beatles, Michelle:*
"Sont des mots qui vont très bien ensemble, très bien ensemble."

⌒

"You and me and Leslie."

—*The Rascals, Groovin':*
"You and me endlessly . . ."

⌒

"I'll be your xylophone waiting for you."

—*The Foundations, Build Me Up Buttercup:*
"I'll be beside the phone waiting for you."

⌒

"Are you going to starve an old friend?"
>   —*Simon and Garfunkel, Scarborough Fair:*
>   *"Are you going to Scarborough Fair?"*

"Baking carrot biscuits."
>   —*Bachman-Turner Overdrive, Taking Care of Business:*
>   *"Taking care of business."*

"Donuts make my brown eyes blue."
>   —*Crystal Gale, Don't It Make My Brown Eyes Blue:*
>   *"Don't it make my brown eyes blue."*

"Got a lot of lucky peanuts."

>> —*Frankie Vallee and the Four Seasons, Let's Hang On:*
>> *"Got a lot of love between us."*

"Hope the city voted for you."

>> —*Grease, Hopelessly Devoted to You:*
>> *"Hopelessly devoted to you."*

"I'm a pool hall ace."

>> —*The Police, Every Step You Take:*
>> *"My poor heart aches."*

"Just brush my teeth before you leave me."

> —*Juice Newton, Angel of the Morning:*
> *"Just touch my cheek before you leave me."*

VI

A BOUQUET
OF
BLOOMING
IDIOTS

THE LAW IS AN ASS: WACKY TESTIMONY

Believe it or not, the following exchanges are gleaned from stenographers' reports of actual court cases.

Attorney: Doctor, how many autopsies have you performed on dead people?

Witness: All my autopsies are performed on dead people.

Attorney: Do you recall the time that you examined the body?

Witness: The autopsy started around 8:30 P.M.

Attorney: And Mr. Dennington was dead at the time?

Witness: No, he was sitting on the table wondering why I was doing an autopsy.

Attorney: Doctor, before you performed the autopsy, did you check for a pulse?

Witness: No.

Attorney: Did you check for blood pressure?

Witness: No.

Attorney: Did you check for breathing?

Witness: No.

Attorney: So, then it is possible that the patient was alive when
             you began the autopsy?
Witness: No.
Attorney: How can you be so sure, Doctor?
Witness: Because his brain was sitting on my desk in a jar.
Attorney: But could the patient have still been alive nevertheless?
Witness: It is possible that he could have been alive and
             practicing law somewhere.

Attorney: What is your date of birth?
Witness: July fifteenth.
Attorney: What year?
Witness: Every year.

Attorney: This myasthenia gravis—does it affect your memory at all?

Witness: Yes.

Attorney: And in what ways does it affect your memory?

Witness: I forget.

Attorney: You forget. Can you give us an example of something that you've forgotten?

Attorney: Now, isn't it true that when a person dies in his sleep, he doesn't know about it until the next morning?

Witness: Sure, I played for ten years. I even went to school for it.

Attorney: You were there until the time you left, is that true?

Attorney: So the date of your baby's conception was August 8th?
Witness: Yes.
Attorney: And what were you doing at that time?

Attorney: How far apart were the vehicles at the time of the collision?

Attorney: What did the tissue samples taken from the victim's vagina show?
Witness: There were traces of semen.
Attorney: Male semen?

Attorney: You say the stairs went down to the basement?
Witness: Yes.
Attorney: And these stairs, did they go up also?

Attorney: Did you ever sleep with him in New York?
Witness: I refuse to answer that question.
Attorney: Did you ever sleep with him in Chicago?
Witness: I refuse to answer that question.
Attorney: Did you ever sleep with him in Miami?
Witness: No.

Attorney: Is your appearance here this morning pursuant to a
           deposition notice which I sent to your attorney?
Witness: No, this is how I dress when I go to work.

Attorney: So, after the anesthetic, when you came out of it, what did you observe with respect to your scalp?

Witness: I didn't see my scalp the whole time I was in the hospital.

Attorney: It was covered?

Witness: Yes. Bandaged.

Attorney: Then, later on, what did you see?

Witness: I had a skin graft. My whole buttocks and leg were removed and put on top of my head.

Clerk: Please repeat after me: "I swear by Almighty God . . ."

Witness: "I swear by Almighty God."

Clerk: "That the evidence that I give . . ."

Witness: That's right.

Clerk: Repeat it.

Witness: "Repeat it."

Clerk: No! Repeat what I said.

Witness: What you said when?

Clerk: "That the evidence that I give . . ."

Witness: "That the evidence that I give."

Clerk:	"Shall be the truth and . . ."
Witness:	It will, and nothing but the truth!
Clerk:	Please, just repeat after me: "Shall be the truth and . . ."
Witness:	I'm not a scholar, you know.
Clerk:	We can appreciate that. Just repeat after me: "Shall be the truth and . . ."
Witness:	"Shall be the truth and."
Clerk:	Say: "Nothing. . . ."
Witness:	Okay. (Witness remains silent.)
Clerk:	No! Don't say nothing. Say: "Nothing but the truth . . ."
Witness:	Yes.
Clerk:	Can't you say: "Nothing but the truth . . . ?"
Witness:	Yes.
Clerk:	Well? Do so.
Witness:	You're confusing me.
Clerk:	Just say: "Nothing but the truth . . ."
Witness:	Is that all?
Clerk:	Yes.
Witness:	Okay. I understand.
Clerk:	Then say it.
Witness:	What?

Clerk: "Nothing but the truth . . ."
Witness: But I do! That's just it.
Clerk: You must say: "Nothing but the truth . . ."
Witness: I WILL say nothing but the truth!
Clerk: Please, just repeat these four words: "Nothing," "But," "The," "Truth."
Witness: What? You mean, like, now?
Clerk: Yes! Now. Please. Just say those four words.
Witness: "Nothing. But. The. Truth."
Clerk: Thank you.
Witness: I'm just not a scholar.

Judge: I simply do not understand why you named this child— his legal name is Weatherby Dot Com Channel Fourcast Sheppard. Now, before you answer that, Mr.— the plaintiff in this action is a weatherman for a local television station?
Plaintiff: Sheppard: Yes.
Judge: Okay. Is that why you named this child the name that you gave the child?

Plaintiff: It—it stems from a lot of things.

Judge: Okay. Tell me what they are.

Plaintiff: Weatherby—I've always heard of Weatherby as a last name and never a first name, so I thought Weatherby would be—and I'm sure you could spell it b-e-e or b-e-a or b-y. Anyway, Weatherby.

Judge: Where did you get the "Dot Com"?

Plaintiff: Well, when I worked at NBC, I worked on a Teleprompter computer.

Judge: All right.

Plaintiff: All right, and so that's where the Dot Com [came from]. I just thought it was kind of cute, Dot Com, and then instead of—I really didn't have a whole lot of names because I had nothing to work with. I don't know family names. I don't know any names of the Speir family, and I really had nothing to work with, and I thought "Channel"? No, that's stupid, and I thought "Shanel," I've heard of a black little girl named Shanel.

Judge: Well, where did you get "Fourcast"?

Plaintiff: Fourcast? Instead of F-o-r-e, like your future forecast or your weather forecast, F-o-u, as in my fourth son, my fourth child, Fourcast. It was—

Judge:	So his name is Fourcast, F-o-u-r-c-a-s-t?
Plaintiff:	Yes.
Judge:	All right. Now, do you have some objection to him being renamed Samuel Charles?
Plaintiff:	Yes.
Judge:	Why? You think it's better for his name to be Weatherby Dot Com Channel—
Plaintiff:	Well, the—
Judge:	Just a minute for the record.
Plaintiff:	Sorry.
Judge:	Channel Fourcast, spelled F-o-u-r-c-a-s-t? And in response to that question, I want you to think about what he's going to be—what his life is going to be like when he enters the first grade and has to fill out all [the] paperwork where you fill out—this little kid fills out his last name and his first name and his middle name, okay? So I just want—if your answer to that is yes, you think his name is better today than it would be with Samuel Charles, as his father would like to name him and why. Go ahead.
Plaintiff:	Yes, I think it's better this way.
Judge:	The way he is now?

Plaintiff: Yes. He doesn't have to use "Dot Com." I mean, as a grown man, he can use whatever he wants.

Judge: As a grown man, what is his middle name? Dot Com Channel Fourcast?

Plaintiff: He can use Channel, he can use the letter "C."

Judge: And when he gives his birth certificate—is it on his birth certificate as you've stated to Judge? Does his birth—does this child's birth certificate read "Weatherby Dot Com"—

Plaintiff: That's how I filled out the paperwork for his—

Judge: —Channel Fourcast?

Plaintiff: Yes, and for his Social Security card, I filled it out as Weatherby F. Sheppard.

The Court: All right.

Bear To The Right:
Questions Asked at National Parks

꙳ Is the mule train air-conditioned?

꙳ What time does the two o'clock bus leave?

꙳ Can you show me where the yeti lives?

꙳ How often do you mow the tundra?

꙳ How much does Mount McKinley weigh?

꙳ Did people build this, or did Indians?

෬ Why did they build the ruins so close to the road?

෬ Do you know of any undiscovered ruins?

෬ Why did the Indians decide to live in Colorado?

෬ How much of the cave is underground?

෬ So what's in the unexplored part of the cave?

෬ Where are the cages for the animals?

෬ What time do you turn on Yosemite Falls?

෬ Was this [the Grand Canyon] man-made?

○ [at Everglades National Park] Are the alligators real?

○ [at Mount Rushmore] Can I get my picture taken with the carving of President Clinton?

○ Does Old Faithful erupt at night?

○ How do you turn [Old Faithful] on?

○ When does the guy who turns [Old Faithful] on get to sleep?

○ We had no trouble finding the park entrances, but where are the exits?

WHERE AM I?: TOURIST QUESTIONS ASKED AT VISITORS BUREAUS

∽ Do you have a map of the Iditarod Trail? We'd like to go for a walk now.

∽ Which beach is closest to the water?

∽ Have we made peace with the Indians?

∽ Where can we find Amish hookers? We want to buy a quilt.

∽ What is the official language of Alaska?

∾ What's the best time of year to watch deer turn into elk?

∾ Where are Scarlet and Rhett buried and are they buried together?

∾ If you go to a restaurant in Idaho and you don't want any kind of potato with your meal, will they ask you to leave?

∾ I am trying to build a flying saucer. Where do I go for help?

∾ Where can I find a listing of jazz funerals for the month?

SELECTED QUOTED SOURCES

Acfield, David, Twentieth-century British cricket player

Agassiz, Louis (1807–1873), Swiss-American zoologist and geologist

Agnew, Spiro (1918–1996), Vice President of the United States

Alario, John D., Louisiana state senator and state representative

Alexander, Avery, Louisiana state representative

Allen, Richard, national security advisor to Ronald Reagan

Alliss, Peter (b. 1931), German-American golf commentator

Anderson, Kim, mayor of Naples, Florida

Andujar, Joaquin (b. 1972), National League pitcher

Aspel, Michael (b. 1933), British television personality

Atkinson, Ron (b. 1939), British soccer player and commentator

Aubrey, John (1626–1697), English antiquary and writer

Babbage, Charles (1792–1871), English mathematician and inventor

Bakker, James (b. 1941), American preacher and televangelist

Banks, Sir Joseph (1743–1820), English explorer and president of the British Royal Society

Barry, Marion (b. 1936), Democratic mayor of Washington, D.C.

Bayh, Evan (b. 1955), Democratic senator from Indiana

Beck, Barry (b. 1957), New York Rangers hockey player

Benaud, Richie (b. 1930), Australian cricket commentator

Bennett, Winston (b. 1965), University of Kentucky basketball forward

Benton, Barbi, American model and actress

Berra, Yogi (b. 1925), American baseball player for the New York Yankees

Bevin, Ernest (1881–1951), British labor leader and foreign minister

Blackman, Paul, research coordinator at the National Rifle Association

Blofeld, Henry (b. 1939), British cricket player and commentator

Blyth, Chay (b. 1940), British rower who crossed the Atlantic in a rowboat

Boxer, Barbara (b. 1940), U.S. senator from California

Boylston, Zabdiel (1679–1766), American physician

Bradshaw, Terry (b. 1948), NFL football player and broadcaster

Brand, Othal, member of a Texas pesticide review board

Bridges, Rocky (b. 1927), American baseball player and manager

Bruno, Frank (b. 1961), English heavyweight boxer

Bryant, Anita (b. 1940), American singer

Budd, Zola (b. 1966), South African record-setting barefoot runner

Burke, Tim (b. 1959), Montreal Expos pitcher

Bush, Earl, press aide to Chicago mayor Richard Daley

Bush, George H. W. (b.1924), Forty-first President of the United States

Bush, George W. (b. 1946), Forty-third President of the United States

Bush, Jeb (b. 1953), governor of Florida and brother of President George W. Bush

Bush, Vannevar (1890–1974), American electrical engineer and physicist

Carey, Mariah (b. 1970), American singer

Cavett, Dick (b. 1936), American television entertainer

Chaney, Darrel (b. 1948), Atlanta Braves infielder

Chaplin, Charlie (1889–1977), English silent film actor

Chrétien, Jean (b. 1934), Prime Minister of Canada

Churchill, Winston (1871–1947), American novelist

Clarke, Arthur C. (b. 1917), British science fiction writer

Clinton, Bill (b. 1946), Forty-second President of the United States

Clinton, Hillary (b. 1947), U.S. First Lady and Senator

Coble, Howard, North Carolina representative

Coe, Sebastian (b. 1956), British Olympic track runner and member of
   Parliament

Coleman, Clarence "Choo Choo" (b. 1937), New York Mets baseball player

Coleman, David, British sports commentator

Coleman, Jerry (b. 1924), New York Yankees infielder and baseball
   commentator

Connally, John (1917–1993), Secretary of the Treasury under President
   Richard M. Nixon

Coolidge, Calvin (1872–1933), Thirtieth President of the United States

Cooper, Gary (1901–1961), American movie actor

Crozier, Tony, British sports commentator

Daley, Richard J. (1902–1976), mayor of Chicago

Dark, Alvin (b. 1922), New York Giants infielder

Darman, Richard (b. 1944), director of the U.S. Office of Management
   and Budget under President George H. W. Bush

Daschle, Tom (b. 1947), senator from South Dakota

Davies, Barry, British soccer commentator

Davis, Ron (b. 1955), Minnesota Twins pitcher

Dawson, Andre (b. 1954), Chicago Cubs outfielder

de Angelis, Augustin, Seventeenth-century Italian friar of the Clementine
   College

de Forest, Lee (1873–1961), American inventor in the field and wireless
    communication

de Gaulle, Charles (1890–1970), President of France

de Lesseps, Ferdinand Marie (1805–1894), French diplomat and engineer

Dean, Dizzy (1911–1974), American baseball player

Dean, W. W., Early twentieth-century president of Dean Telephone
    Company

Diez, Juba, Louisiana state representative

Dinkins, David (b. 1927), mayor of New York City

Dodd, Christopher (b. 1944), U.S. senator from Connecticut

Dole, Bob (b. 1923), U.S. senator and 1996 presidential candidate

Drake, Edwin L. (1819–1880), American oil well driller

Duell, Charles H., commissioner, U.S. Office of Patents

Duva, Lou (b. 1922), American boxing trainer

Early, Joe, U.S. congressman from Massachusetts

Edison, Thomas A. (1847–1931), American inventor

Einhorn, Eddie, owner of the Chicago White Sox baseball team

Eisenhower, Dwight D. (1890–1969), Thirty-fourth President of the
    United States

Ellsworth, Henry L. (1791–1858), American agriculturist and U.S.
    Commissioner of Patents

Enderbery, Keppel, Australian cabinet minister

Ericksen, Sir John Eric, British surgeon

Eubank, Chris (b. 1966), British boxer

Evangelista, Linda (b. 1965), American model

Fairly, Ron (b. 1938), American baseball player and commentator

Ferguson, Miriam Amanda "Ma" (1875–1961), governor of Texas

Fields, Debbi, founder of Mrs. Fields Cookies

Finks, Jim (1927–1994), general manager of the New Orleans Saints
football team

Fisher, Irving (1867–1947), American economist and Yale University
professor

Foch, Ferdinand (1851–1929), French general during World War I

Ford, Gerald R. (b. 1913), Thirty-eight President of the United States

Ford, Henry (1863–1947), American industrialist and automobile
manufacturer

Fowler, Mark S., chairman of the Federal Communications Commission

Francis, Gerry (b. 1951), British soccer player and manager

Francombe, John (b. 1952), jockey and horse racing announcer

French, Ray, rugby sportscaster

Fuentes, Tito (b. 1944), Cuban-American baseball player

Galilei, Galileo (1564–1642), Italian astronomer and physicist

Gobel, George (1920–1991), American comedian and television personality

Goddard, Robert (1882–1945), American physicist and rocket scientist

Goldwyn, Samuel (1882–1974), Polish-American film producer

Gomez, Lefty (1908–1989), American pitcher for the New York Yankees

Gore, Al (b. 1948), Vice President of the United States

Gowdy, Curt (b. 1919), baseball and sports radio commentator

Gratton, Mike, British marathon runner

Greenspan, Alan (b. 1926), chairman of the Federal Reserve

Greenwell, Mike (b. 1963), Boston Red Sox outfielder

Grimson, Stu, Chicago Blackhawks hockey player

Guerrero, Pedro (b. 1956), Los Angeles Dodgers baseball player

Guggenheim, Harry (1890–1971), American diplomat and publisher

Hadley, Stephen, British show jumper

Haldeman, Harry Robbins (1926–1993), American businessman and aide
    to President Richard M. Nixon

Hall, Bridget, American model

Harvey, William (1578–1657), English physician

Hatch, Orrin (b. 1934), U.S. senator from Utah

Hayakawa, S. I., U.S. Senator

Hecht, Chic, Nevada senator and U.S. ambassador to the Bahamas

Helms, Jesse (b. 1921), U.S. senator from North Carolina

Hemond, Roland (b. 1929), Chicago White Sox general manager

Herzog, Frank, Washington sports announcer

Hickel, Walter (b. 1919), U.S. Secretary of the Interior and governor
of Alaska

Hingis, Martina (b. 1980), tennis player

Hitler, Adolf (1889–1945), German dictator and founder of the Nazi party

Hogan, John, Commonwealth Edison supervisor of news information

Hoke, Martin, U.S. representative from Ohio

Hoover, J. Edgar (1895–1972), director of the Federal Bureau of
Investigation

Iacocca, Lee (b. 1924), former chairman of Ford Motor Company

Illingworth, Ray (b. 1932), British cricket player

Jenner, Edward (1749–1823), English physician and smallpox researcher

Jobs, Steve (b. 1955), American founder of Apple Computer, Inc.

Johnson, Earvin "Magic" (b. 1959), Los Angeles Lakers basketball player

Johnson, Lyndon B. (1908–1973), Thirty-sixth President of the
United States

Johnstone, Derek, soccer commentator for BBC Scotland

Jones, Arthur, inventor of Nautilus weight-training equipment

Jones, Peter, British soccer commentator

Kelvin, William (1824–1907), British mathematician and physicist

Kennedy, John F. (1917–1963), Thirty-fifth President of the United States

Kidd, Jason, American basketball player

Kiner, Ralph (b. 1922), American baseball player and New York Mets announcer

King, Ross, track and field commentator

Kulwicki, Alan (1954–1993), American NASCAR stock car racer

Laidlaw, Renton, British golf journalist and writer

Leahy, William (1875–1959), American naval officer and diplomat

Lewis, Gib, Texas Speaker of the House

Licht, Frank, governor of Rhode Island

Lincoln, Abraham (1809–1865), Sixteenth President of the United States

Lindbergh, Charles A. (1902–1974), American aviator

Lindley, Jimmy (b. 1935), British jockey

Loes, Billy (b. 1929), Brooklyn Dodgers pitcher

Lonsborough, Anita, British swimming commentator

Lowe, Ted, British billiards commentator

Lyons, Mick (b. 1951), British soccer player

Macaskill, Ian, BBC weather reporter

Mach, Ernst (1838–1916), Austrian physicist and philosopher

Machin, Stewart, horse race commentator

Maddox, Lester (b. 1915), governor of Georgia

Malavasi, Ray, coach of the St. Louis Rams football team

Malone, Moses (b. 1955), Philadelphia 76ers basketball player

Marx, Groucho (1890–1977), American comedian and actor

Mattingly, Don (b. 1961), New York Yankees infielder

McCarthy, Joseph R. (1908–1957), U.S. senator famous for his anti-Communist campaigns

McDuffie, George (1790–1851), U.S. senator

McGovern, George (b. 1922), U.S. senator from South Dakota

McGraw, Frank "Tug" (1944–2004), National League pitcher

McMains, Chuck, Louisiana state representative

Mecham, Evan, governor of Arizona

Menino, Thomas, mayor of Boston

Minter, Alan (b. 1951), British middleweight boxer

Monks, John, Oklahoma state representative

Moore, Brian (1921–1999), Canadian-American novelist

Morse, Samuel F. B. (1791–1872), American inventor and developer of the telegraph

Moss, Kate (b. 1974), American model

Mountbatten, Philip (b. 1921), husband of Queen Elizabeth II of England

Muhammad, Murad, U.S. boxing promoter

Nel, Louis, South African deputy foreign minister

Nevitt, Chuck (b. 1959), North Carolina State basketball player

Nissalke, Tom, coach of the Houston Rockets basketball team

Nixon, Richard (1913–1994), Thirty-seventh President of the United States

Norman, Greg (b. 1955), Australian golfer

North, Oliver (b. 1943), American Marine colonel and radio host

Ohm, Georg Simon (1787–1854), German physicist

Olson, Ken, president, chairman, and founder of Digital Equipment Corp.

O'Malley, Des, Irish government minister

O'Neal, Shaquille (b. 1972), Los Angeles Lakers basketball player

O'Neill, Paul (b. 1935), Secretary of the Treasury

Opfer, David, U.S. Air Force Colonel

Ozark, Danny (b. 1923), manager of the Philadelphia Phillies baseball team

Pachet, Pierre, professor of physiology at Toulouse

Pascoe, Alan (b. 1947), British track runner

Pasteur, Louis (1822–1895), French chemist

Patten, Chris (b. 1944), conservative British politician

Peterson, Bill, coach of the Florida State football team

Philip, Prince, *See* Mountbatten, Philip

Pickering, Ron, British track commentator

Pierre, Wilfred, Louisiana representative

Polk, Torrin, University of Houston receiver

Power, Francis Gary, American U-2 reconnaissance pilot held by the
Soviets for spying

Preece, Sir Arthur, Nineteenth-century engineer-in-chief of the British
Post Office

Quayle, Dan (b. 1947), Vice President of the United States

Quayle, Marilyn, wife of Dan Quayle

Rappaport, Dennis, American boxing manager

Reagan, Nancy (b. 1923), U.S. First Lady

Reagan, Ronald (1911–2004), Fortieth President of the United States

Resch, Chico (b. 1948), Canadian-born New York Islanders hockey goalie

Rice, Condoleezza (b. 1954), U.S. national security advisor

Rickenbacker, Eddie (1890–1973), American aviator and airline executive

Rivers, Mickey (b. 1948), Texas Rangers outfielder

Rizzuto, Phil (b. 1918), Yankees baseball player and announcer

Robson, Bryan (b. 1957), British soccer player

Roche, Sir Boyle, Eighteenth-century Irishman

Rogers, George (b. 1958), New Orleans Saints running back

Roosevelt, Franklin D. (1882–1945), Thirty-second President of the
United States

Rose, Pete (b. 1941), American baseball player

Rumsfeld, Donald (b. 1932), Secretary of Defense

Rutherford, Sir Ernest (1871–1937), British nuclear physicist

Rutigliano, Sam, Cleveland Browns coach

Sarnoff, David (1891–1971), Russian-American radio and television
    executive

Scheibel, Jim, mayor of St. Paul, Minnesota

Schiffer, Claudia (b. 1970), American model

Schwarzenegger, Arnold (b. 1947), Austrian-American actor and governor
    of California

Scott, William (1867–1934), U.S. Representative and Senator from
    Pennsylvania

Shackleford, Charles (b. 1966), North Carolina State player

Sheridan, Richard (1751–1816), English dramatist and politician

Shields, Brooke (b. 1965), American actress

Silver, Spencer, inventor of Post-It® notes

Sinatra, Frank (1915–1998), American singer and actor

Smiles, Samuel (1812–1904), Scottish political reformer

Smith, David, British curling commentator

Smith, Fred, founder of Federal Express

Smith, Harvey, British show jumper

Smith, Ian (b. 1919), Rhodesian political leader

Smuts, General Jan Christiaan (1870–1950), South African statesman and soldier

Smyth, Sir John (1554–1612), English nonconformist clergyman

Spooner, Rev. W. A., (1844–1930), British lecturer

Stalin, Joseph (1879–1973), Soviet Communist leader

Starmer-Smith, Nigel, English rugby player and writer

Stengel, Casey (1871–1975), American baseball player and scanner

Stephanopoulos, George (b. 1961), political adviser to Bill Clinton

Stephenson, George (1781–1848), English engineer

Stokes, George Gabriel (1819–1903), British mathematician and physicist, chairman of British Leyland

Streifer, Philip, superintendent of schools, Barrington, Rhode Island

Summers, Lawrence (b. 1954), American chief economist of the World Bank

Swinburn, Walter, British jockey

Symonds, Sir William, surveyor of the British Navy

Thach, Nguyen Co, Vietnamese foreign minister

Theismann, Joe (b. 1946), NFL football quarterback

Thomas, Isaiah (b. 1961), NBA basketball player and coach

Thomas, Lowell (1892–1981), American radio announcer

Toiv, Barry, White House deputy press secretary under Bill Clinton

Travis, John, Louisiana state representative

Tredgold, Thomas (1788–1829), engineering writer

Trollope, Anthony (1815–1882), English novelist

Trotsky, Leon (1879–1940), Russian Communist revolutionary

Trump, Donald (b. 1946), American business executive

Tyson, Mike (b. 1966), American boxer

Vanik, Charles (b. 1913), U.S. representative from Ohio

Velpeau, Alfred (1795–1867), French surgeon

Walker, Johnny, world middleweight wrist-wrestling champion

Walker, Murray, car racing announcer and writer

Wallace, George (1919–1998), governor of Alabama

Warner, Harry (1881–1958), co-founder of Warner Brothers movie studio

Watson, Thomas John Sr., (1874–1956), founder and chairman of IBM

Watt, James, Secretary of the Interior

Wayne, John (1907–1979), American film actor

Weld, William, (b. 1945), governor of Massachusetts

Wellman, Gerald, ROTC instructor

Westinghouse, George (1846–1914), American inventor and manufacturer

Westmoreland, General William (b. 1914), U.S. Army Chief of Staff

Westwood, Lee (b. 1973), British golfer

White, Fred, announcer for the Kansas City Royals baseball team

Wiley, Alexander, U.S. senator from Wisconsin

Willard-Lewis, Cynthia, Louisiana state representative

Williams, Dorian, British horse show commentator

Williams, Venus (b. 1980), American tennis player

Wolfe-Barry, Sir John (1836–1919), English civil engineer

Wollaston, William H. (1766–1828), English scientist

Wood, Leon (b. 1976), New Jersey Nets basketball player

Woodroofe, Tommy, Lieutenant Commander of the Royal Navy

Woodward, Clark, U.S. Rear Admiral in World War II

Wozniak, Steve (b. 1950), American computer industry pioneer

Zanuck, Darryl (1902–1979), head of 20th Century Fox movie studios